QUICK HITS

QUICK HITS

Successful Strategies by Award Winning Teachers

Edited by:
Eileen Bender
Millard Dunn
Bonnie Kendall
Catherine Larson
Peggy Wilkes

INDIANA UNIVERSITY PRESS
BLOOMINGTON◆INDIANAPOLIS

The paper used in this publication meets the minimum requirements of American National Standard for Information Sciences—Permanence of Paper for Printed Library Materials, ANSI Z39.48-1984.

Manufactured in the United States of America

Library of Congress Cataloging-in-Publication Data

Quick hits : successful strategies by award winning teachers / edited
  by Eileen Bender, Millard Dunn, Bonnie Kendall, Catherine Larson,
  Peggy Wilkes.
      p.   cm.
    ISBN 0-253-20923-4
    1. College teaching—Indiana. 2. College teachers—Indiana.
  3. Indiana University—Faculty. I. Bender, Eileen.
  LB2331.Q53 1994
  378.1'25'09772ESS—dc 20   94-3693

        3 4 5 00 99 98

CONTENTS

Philosophies of Teaching and Learning 58

Writing 64

Exams 73

Teaching Non-Traditional Adult Learners 77

A Sense of Humor 78

Class Conduct 81

Electronic Classroom 86

Moments . . . 89

Contributors 91

PREFACE

Quick Hits was invented at an annual retreat of FACET (Faculty Colloquium on Excellence in Teaching) as a way for Indiana University's most talented teachers to exchange their ideas for improving classroom performance. It has become a regular feature of FACET, established in 1989, to recognize and support distinguished teaching faculty from each of Indiana University's eight campuses, and to provide a forum for the discussion of teaching and university policy.

As I write these words, I cannot help smiling, for I have just wrapped up the paper work from the summer session class I taught. This course, an Intensive Freshman Seminar, met three hours a day, five days a week for three weeks. The students enrolled in it were all incoming freshmen, seventeen and eighteen year olds, for whom this was the maiden voyage on the seas of higher education. The duration and pacing of the class, the attention span and anxiety of the students, the newness of the subject matter initially looked to me like a recipe for burn-out, but my students and I arrived on the last day exhilarated rather than exhausted.

I owe much of this success to the contributors of Quick Hits. Under rigorous conditions, I can testify that they work. They work very well.

The idea for Quick Hits originated at the third FACET retreat, which focussed on practical as well as theoretical aspects of teaching. The new FACET inductees were invited to bring their favorite teaching strategies and explain or demonstrate them to the other participants in three to five minute segments tucked between longer workshops. The program planners for FACET III perceived the Quick Hits sessions as fulfilling three important functions: first, they provided people with a way to learn each other's names and disciplines; second, they provided an opportunity for people to shine before an appreciative audience; third, they taught everyone something to incorporate into and improve their own practice. The Quick Hits sessions were so lively and entertaining that they became a permanent feature of FACET retreats, but, more importantly, they were so valuable that they launched the FACET publication series as well.

FACET's spirit is embodied in the phrase Each One Teach One. We are a grassroots movement dedicated to getting better at what we do. Quick Hits is an offering we make to each other in that spirit. We all understand that we have much to learn; we all understand that what we give away is repaid many times over; we all recognize our enormous debt to each other.

Bonnie Kendall
Anthropology
IU Bloomington

FIRST
DAYS

"Personalized interaction is lasting."
Vince Peterson

Ignorance Is An Equal Opportunity Experience

"We're all ignorant, just about different things," Will Rogers said. I say it at the start of every semester in nearly every class I teach. Why? Because in this age of hyper-specialization, we academics can hardly keep up with our own research areas, let alone our own disciplines or related disciplines. In this era of rapidly advancing knowledge, the "truth" of our own doctoral exams quickly becomes the "falsehood" of our students'. In this age of multiple disciplines and multiple media and data systems, people are simply exposed to different bodies of knowledge and information.

"Expert" though we academics may be, ignorance is not something students have and faculty don't. It is not something that humanists suffer from and scientists don't. It is not the exclusive province of conservatives - or liberals.

"Expert" though we academics may be, ignorance is not something students have and faculty don't. It is not something that humanists suffer from and scientists don't. It is not the exclusive province of conservatives - or liberals.

Ignorance is an equal opportunity experience. And if recognized and openly acknowledged as such, it can be a catalyst for true collaborative learning - the kind of learning in which students learn from teachers, students learn from other students, and teachers learn as much from students as students learn from them.

Holly Stocking
Journalism
IU Bloomington

Ice Breaking Demo

I follow this simple rule: different strokes for different folks. For different classes I have tried varied activities on the first day. In some classes I give quizzes. Students recover from the shock after I tell them that the grade will not count in their final grade and that this is simply a diagnostic test. Quiz results enable me to reach a larger number of students.

I don't forget to let my students know that I do care about their progress and success; and I am willing to go the extra mile for them if they are ready to work hard.

Normally, however, I use a good and appropriate lecture demonstration to raise simple questions suitable for the first day of class. One such example is converting copper into silver or gold. This is accomplished by heating zinc powder and 10% sodium hydroxide solution first, then placing a small piece of copper wire in it. The copper wire becomes silvery white (ask if this is real? or magic? or science?). If the wire is washed and heated in a flame, it turns to a golden color. This provides a discussion of science, and scientific methods. Other fun and thought-provoking demonstrations are also used on the first day. Occasionally, I use simple toys that will serve a similar purpose. The name of the game is breaking the ice and crossing the barrier between student and teacher. The discussion of the syllabus, grading and general policies follow this awakening experience.

I don't forget to let my students know that I do care about their progress and success; and I am willing to go the extra mile for them if they are ready to work hard.

Kris Dhawale
Chemistry
IU East

Democracy in the Classroom

By letting students choose the number of quizzes, exams, and papers required, they are far less likely to complain. More importantly, it gives them a sense of ownership in both the class and the evaluation process.

I make a point of indicating the pros and cons of different combinations, including which options take more work for both parties. I also point out that their learning is highly correlated to class effort. Therefore, if they are willing to put in the extra effort of frequent evaluations (usually quizzes), then I am willing to put in the corresponding additional effort of creating and grading the quizzes. During the first class, I also tell them that if they haven't reached a two-thirds majority agreement by the second class meeting, I will impose my preferences. Even though this would be the case without classroom democracy, they seem to interpret it in a rather terrified manner. Based on students' comments, most value this technique.

Patrick Rooney
Economics
IU Columbus

Video Journal

On the first day of class I sometimes bring a video camera, particularly if the class is a large one. I film each student for about 10 seconds (they like the attention; it's a good ice breaker, and it takes surprisingly little time). I then digitize the pictures into the computer to create a computer photo book, which turns out to be a great reference manual for me. First, it helps me to learn the students' names; secondly, it helps me recall students years later when they ask for letters of recommendation or I receive mail from them. With my photo album, I can quickly retrieve associations.

James Mumford
Afro-American Arts Institute
IU Bloomington

"Families"

Divide the class in half, then have students select a partner they don't know from the opposite half. Ask them to find out everything they can about this person in five minutes. Next, partners are joined to make four, and told they are "families" for the rest of the semester. Students sign their names on a document, one for each family, and then maintains a folder with their signatures attached. I use "families" in wholes, parts or paired for discussions and exercises.

I hand out 4 x 6 note cards to each "family" for the "Ideal Me" assignment. Students write key words representing qualities that they believe essential in themselves, a preschool child, or some other age group. On a huge sketch of a person, I write the words. That helps them to realize the impossibility of such a person.

This is followed by the "Ideal Professor Wagor" assignment about qualities they want to find in me in this course. I write these on the board and explain how I need to be myself rather than fulfill all of their expectations, which helps get their expectations out in the open.

Walter Wagor
Psychology
IU East

A Collage of Thinking

I start the first class by asking my students what they know about a topic. I then put their answers together to create a collage of thinking and knowledge.

At the end of the semester (or even during the semester), I ask students to revisit their original thoughts to see if they still feel the same.

FACET Alumnus
Lilly House Conference
September, 1991

Developing a Checklist

Prepare a checklist for students so they will know what you expect of them. Here's my checklist for my physics course:

HOW TO DO WELL IN THIS CLASS

✔ **How much time do you invest in this class?** An average student who does not naturally take to physics but still gets a grade of B or better, budgets about 12 hours a week.

✔ **Do you come to class?** You'll probably learn something **no matter how bad the instructor is**.

✔ **Do you come prepared?** Stay current. If you are studying Chapter 4 when the lecture is on Chapter 6 you are reinforcing all your anxieties. You do not need perfection. Just do the best you can, but stay with the class.

✔ **When do you study for this class?** Break up your study time. Twenty-four one-hour periods a week (two a day) is best. Don't study when you're tired.

✔ **How do you study?** Study by doing. That means working problems. Go back and forth between the problems, the examples, and the text in the book, in that order.

✔ **Do you work for understanding?** When you get the answer to a problem right (by trial and error, if necessary) go back over the problem to see why the method you employed worked.

✔ **Can you explain it to others?** If possible, work in a group. Explain your solution to others.

✔ **Work on your self- confidence.** Before you look up the answer or the solution, assign a confidence factor to your work. On a scale of 1-10, how confident are you that your solution is right? Be honest with yourself. The more often you prove yourself right, the less test anxiety you'll have.

✔ **Do you cram for tests?** Don't. It will not work. Do not change your study habits because a test is coming. The most usable knowledge is already there. Cramming for tests leads to fatigue, test anxiety, and stupid mistakes.

Unfortunately all this is a lot easier said than done. Good luck!!

Gregor Novak
Physics
IUPUI

Joe Chandler, a colleague at IPFW, begins each class with a "Quote of the Day." He has several of them recorded on large cards which he places on his classroom desk. He varies the quotes to include humorous, philosophical and serious. However, all tend to be motivational messages meant to challenge thinking. The more appropriate the quote is to the day's topic, the more discussion is generated.

Shirley Rickert
Organizational Leadership and Supervision
IP Ft. Wayne

Quote of the Day

In all things: we learn only from those we love.
Goethe

Everything has it's beauty but not everyone sees it. Confucius

The teacher gives not of his wisdom, But rather of his faith and lovingness.
The Prophet
Kahlil Gibran

The secret of education lies in respecting the pupil.
Ralph Waldo Emerson

Caterpillar: ... and who are you?

Alice: ...I...I hardly know, Sir, just at present— at least I know who I was when I got up this morning, but I think I must have changed several times since then.

Lewis Carroll
Alice in Wonderland

Researches I have conducted show that a person will permit himself to be known when he believes his audience is a man of goodwill.
Sidney M. Jourard
The Transparent Self

Their Goals First

Often, the first tangible and enduring interaction our students have with us is our course syllabus. Throughout the past five years, I have made several modifications in my course syllabi designed to reach out to my students, engaging them more directly and immediately. Some may seem trivial; others are obviously more substantive; taken altogether, they illustrate my philosophy of teaching and learning, while concurrently outlining the work of the semester.

1. There is a space for the student's name, a seemingly trivial addition, but one that indicates up front that the syllabus is theirs.

2. After listing my office hours, I urge students to make an appointment, encouraging them to consider times not listed. Throughout the syllabus I mention that my office is open to discuss course goals, activities or assignments. Often, students feel reluctant to come to their professor's office, or to seek an appointment outside regular office hours. Plus, being on a commuter campus makes it especially difficult for students to match their schedules to their professor's office hours.

3. As I outline my course goals and the semester, I leave space for them to write their course goals and their semester's work.

I used to put my goals first, but last year I modified the syllabus to invite their goals first. I tell them it is up to them to ensure that I know what their goals are, and then it is up to me to help them achieve them.

My intention is to set up, right away, an atmosphere of shared involvement and responsibility for making the semester's work successful.

4. I leave blank spaces on the weekly schedule of readings, topics, and assignments so that once we decide who will present when, we all write the student-presenter's names next to the appropriate date. This serves to reinforce each student's class offerings as an integral part of the course.

5. At the end of the syllabus, after I have described the nature and rationale for the course assignments and their grading, I articulate my basic philosophy of teaching, learning, and assessing learning, to invite questions and reactions. In so doing, I try to be "up front" about my expectations for my students, and similarly request they be equally "up front" with their responses and expectations for me.

I think of my syllabus going out to my students and to the community as an ambassador of me, my course, my department, and my campus.

Sharon Hamilton
English
IUPUI

Say "Cheese"

During the first class meeting, I have students write their names on the board in groups of three or four. Then I have them pose under their names for a Polaroid snapshot. This is the surest way to quickly learn names! Some may be a little embarrassed about it, but I promise them that I will learn their names within a week this way. For planning group discussions, I post the photos at the front of the classroom to help students learn each other's names.

Patrick Rooney
Economics
IU Columbus

Professor on the "Hot Seat"

The first day of class is a good time to clarify student and professor expectations. In addition to reviewing the syllabus, it is a good idea to address the subject of what the students expect to gain from the class.

Divide the class into small groups (not more than 7 each), have the groups identify a spokesperson and give them 10 minutes to confer. At the end of 10 minutes, have the groups report round-robin style until all student goals are listed. The professor has recorded the questions and will assess success during an evaluation meeting with the class at the end of the semester.

The second half of the activity is to have the students, in the same groups with selected spokespersons, take 10 minutes to confer on any question they wish to ask the professor. The professor leaves the room during this time. When the professor returns, the questions are asked in round-robin style until all have been asked. The professor answers the questions as they are asked. One proviso is that the professor reserves the right not to answer questions which are deemed inappropriate (e.g., age, sexual preference, etc.).

In the 12 years that I have used this technique, I have never had an inappropriate question. Usually, nearly three-fourths of the questions refer to grading practices, absences and other procedural matters. The few that are personal in nature tend to focus on past work experience, academic qualifications, marital status, number of children, etc.

Shirley Rickert
Organizational Leadership and Supervision
IU Fort Wayne

Interviewing

Nancy Davis, my instructor in Writing for Publication, used this great ice breaker to get our small class going: including Ms. Davis, we arranged our chairs in a circle. Ms. Davis then directed us to interview the person on our left for ten minutes. Although she knew that only a couple of us had interviewing experience, she gave no specific instructions. Next, we were interviewed by the person on our right. Afterwards, each of us introduced the person we had interviewed to the class and related what we had discovered about him/her.

Because only a couple of us followed proper interviewing procedures, the first impressions we received of one another were personal - things we had on our minds. We quickly became comfortable enough among ourselves to critique each other's work and collaborate on group projects.

Peggy Wilkes/FACET
Nontraditional Student
IU Bloomington

Name Game
Adjective Alliteration

With the class seated in a circle, the instructor announces that each person in succession use an adjective that begins with the same sound as the first sound of his/her name (e.g., "Pretty Peggy," "Funny Phyllis"). However, students can't say their name and adjective <u>until</u> they have accurately repeated the name and adjective of <u>each</u> person who has gone before. The person whose name and/or "adjective" cannot be recalled may help the person. Continue until all students have been included. The instructor should begin the activity and also end it by repeating all of the names and adjectives.

Variation:

At the end of the activity, have students switch seats and ask for a volunteer to give each one's adjective and name.

Vince Peterson
Education
IU South Bend

Avoiding the Big

TURN OFF 👎

The first day of class can be absolutely critical to the success of the entire course. The cliche that "first impressions count" is true, and while this may be an unfair judgment, an informal survey of my students indicates that certain impressions can be **instantaneous turn-offs**.

For example, a professor who is well-groomed and neat in appearance will certainly make a favorable first impression. Granted, such posturing has nothing to do with the course content or the scholarly abilities of the professor, but it does become an immediate focus of attention. A professor who is neat and well-groomed is probably organized, takes pride in whatever he or she does, and is setting a professional example for students to emulate. I once knew a professor who wore such loud color combinations that students could not avoid making surreptitious jests about his outfits. Such distractions cannot help but detract from the professor's overall effectiveness.

Another "peeve" that students have is with professors who are **late** for class. We expect students to be on time for each class; professors have an obligation to do the same. Professors who are repeatedly late have, in the students' eyes, little respect for their students as individuals. There will be rare occasions when you will be unavoidably late for the start of your class but do not let the first day of class be one of those occasions.

What you do during that first session is crucial. Distributing copies of your course syllabus and administrative policies, though essential, should not be the sole purpose of the session. While some professors routinely make the first session a **brief** one, such brevity can be perceived as either a lack of preparedness, indifference to the subject or the class, or outright laziness. If you have an **interesting** first session, students certainly will not be marking time until the end of the period. A boring first class is a harbinger of what is to follow.

I involve students in the first class discussion. Involvement is a simple exercise in getting to know one another or something more intellectually stimulating. The involvement and student-professor interaction **is** what is important.

Being on time, being neat and well-groomed, being interesting and being prepared for a full and stimulating first session will cause your students to look forward to further sessions with you. Certainly, you must continue working hard to sustain their interest. But keeping students turned-on is much easier than attempting to capture their interest once they have been turned-off.

Robert Orr
Computer Technology
IUPUI

Direct Communication

A circular seating arrangement is best so that students can talk to each other directly (students will help move desks before and after class). For fairly large classes, a double U arrangement works well. The instructor should sit within the circle to facilitate the process.

Have students write their preferred names on 5 X 7 cards folded lengthwise.

Students in the circular seating arrangement can place the cards on the floor in front of their seats. Students seated around tables should place the cards in front of them.

Encourage students to talk directly to each other, using the other person's name. Personalized interaction is lasting.

Vince Peterson
Education
IU South Bend

Will Class Participation "Kill" You?

The purpose of this activity is to establish a norm of class participation during the first class meeting while introducing some basic principles of research methodology. Many students seem to believe that speaking up in class will "kill" them. This demonstration uses a very simple pretest-posttest design to test in a rational manner this irrational belief right before the student's eyes.

The only thing needed is a balled-up piece of paper.

The following steps each correspond to a basic methodological principle:

Step 1. Statement of rival hypotheses: I'll bet your life I'm right! Start the activity by giving a simple definition of a hypothesis. Then give the following two hypotheses:

Student: Speaking up in class will kill you.

Instructor: Speaking up in class will not kill you.

Tell students that you have such faith in your own hypothesis that you are willing to bet their lives on it.

Step 2. Selection of subjects: Follow the bouncing ball. For large classes, demonstrate the process of randomly selecting subjects. Wad up a piece of paper and throw it out into the classroom or lecture hall. The person who catches it is your first subject. Standing at his or her seat, this person then throws the ball out in any direction, and the next person to catch it is the second subject. (Subjects should remain standing.) Continue this procedure until you feel you have a sample of adequate size. now ask the students to come to the front of the classroom.

Step 3. Pretest measure: Are all of the subjects alive? At this point, the operational definition of "alive" must be clarified because it is imperative that all of the subjects be alive at the start of the demonstration to provide a fair test of the hypotheses. To do this, make the distinction between being "alive" (i.e., thinking and feeling) and being alive but "brain dead." For the purpose of the demonstration, you will want to assume that everyone is both alive and thinking. You can point out that because the subjects were able to follow your directions up to this point, it is safe to assume that all of them fit the operational definition of being alive prior to the introduction of the treatment.

Step 4. Introducing the treatment: Speaking up in front of the class. Ask the students to describe what they feel would be a fair test of which of the two hypotheses is correct. An obvious treatment is to ask the subjects to speak directly to the class, giving their name, proposed major, and something they like to do in their spare time.

Step 5. The posttest measure: Are you still alive? Because nobody actually dies after speaking, the students can conclude that, at least in this course, speaking up in class will not kill you.

You might point out to them that this is an extremely powerful test of the hypothesis. If standing up in front of the entire class will not kill them, surely they are clearly out of danger when speaking from the safety of their desks, surrounded by their friends.

Step 6. A lesson in the formulation of alternative explanations: Suppose somebody did die? To get the students participating immediately in a class discussion, ask them to speculate about what alternative explanations might be used to explain the highly unlikely possibility of someone's actually dying during the demonstration (e.g., selecting a sickly or intoxicated subject). In addition, how would the demonstration have to be modified to control for such explanations, thus providing a more valid test of the hypothesis?

Step 7. A note on ecological validity: See, talking during the discussion did not kill you. Before terminating this activity, you might point out that because those students who participated in the postdemonstration discussion in Step 6 are still alive, you now have further evidence to support the ecological validity of your hypothesis. In addition, to test the generalizability of this conclusion, encourage the students to participate in their other classes as well and report the results back at the next class meeting.

Bernardo Carducci
Psychology
IU Southeast

The Name Game

The Name Game is a collaborative learning exercise which accomplishes a variety of important things:

♡**It makes you learn your students' names quickly and it makes your students learn each other's names quickly.**

♡**It creates a sense of fun and involvement in the early weeks of the semester.**

♡**It demonstrates that collaboration has advantages over working in isolation.**

Lots of professors play a variant of The Name Game, but my version is based on what I call "the group mind" technique. I tell the students that we have three weeks (or three classes or whatever) to learn each other's names and that we are all responsible for insuring that everyone does it. I explain that cultures all over the world have developed strategies for insuring the social distribution of knowledge, such that if one person is lost, the knowledge is retained somewhere else in the group (you can skip this step if you teach, say engineering and don't want to talk about fuzzy stuff like culture). I encourage them to help each other in the learning process.

Start by having seven to ten students introduce themselves and then ask an individual in the group to name other individuals: "Luke, which one of these people is Rick?" "Rick, point to Susan." "Susan, what is the name of the person sitting next to Attila?"

Bonnie Kendall
Anthropology
IU Bloomington

The Name of the Rose

My problem stems from my deeply ingrained bias that teachers teach and students learn. It's only recently that I discovered that we teachers are also the learners and our students the teachers. To establish the full two-way collaboration I find it essential to know each student personally. Of course, I can't, but it's amazing how close I can come. I start with the usual trick of taking a color Polaroid of all my students in groups of five. They immediately put their names on the back for me. That night I arrange the whole class on sheets with names under each person. If I also meet these students in smaller discussion sections, I arrange the pictures by section.

It's only recently that I discovered that we teachers are also the learners and our students the teachers.

For the first few weeks all seems dark and dismal. Even though I study my gallery of pictures before each class, nothing sticks. I hand back graded homework in class wherever possible. As students collaborate in groups I make sure they know each other's names and listen in as they introduce each other. If I don't remember a name, I always ask before every conversation, both in and out of class (It's very embarrassing to have to ask, especially the forty second time!).

Ben Brabson
Physics
IU Bloomington

A Framework for Learning

I don't know how successfully I have handled it, but a perennial challenge in teaching Religious Studies (and above all in teaching the New Testament) is establishing a framework for learning that is at once empathetic and critical. Many of my students come to a course in the NT expecting a confirmation of their religious convictions, often of a very conservative and sometimes a of a militant character; others presume that their professor will be a godless atheist whom they must fight. Still others are disaffected from their own religious traditions, or hostile to religion in general. Their expectation of a religious studies professor in a state university is that she or he will be interested in demolishing traditional beliefs.

From the start, I deal with expectation/bias, acknowledge the issues that are at stake, and invite students into a shared discussion in which everyone's starting point will in some fashion be changed.

With these expectations, teaching a course in "Jesus Traditions" is a genuine challenge.

Therefore, from the start, I deal with expectation/bias, acknowledge the issues that are at stake, and invite the students into a shared discussion in which everyone's starting point will in some fashion be changed. I also encourage a set of what I call "intellectual virtues" which should characterize debate within the humanities.

I guess this has been fairly successful, since I have had few of the sorts of confrontations that folk in my field often experience, and I have the sense that the class atmosphere is one in which genuine learning is taking place.

Luke Johnson
Religious Studies
IU Bloomington

Using Magazines to Generate Discussion

Bring magazines to the first session. Lots of them! More than the number of students by a factor of 1.5 or 2. Spread them around the room on the floor. Have students choose a magazine and find a picture that appeals to them for any reason at all.

Have each student pair off with someone he or she doesn't know or knows least well in the class. Have the students decide who is A and who is B.

A begins by telling B about the picture and must continue talking until the instructor signals to stop. the rule is that A <u>must continue to talk!</u> Instruct A to talk about anything at all after thoughts about the picture are exhausted. Just keep talking.

B merely listens and nods approval and says nothing more than an occasional "uh-huh." B's role is to listen and remember what he or she heard.

After eight or ten minutes, the instructor signals "stop." B's role becomes that of restating as accurately as possible everything she remembers about A's comments. <u>Accuracy</u> is the key word: no editorializing or analyzing. B merely repeats to A.

Then A and B switch roles.

Lastly, they discuss how well they think each of them performed as listeners and why they were asked to utilize the pictures rather than merely strike up a conversation.

Important Tips:

Really emphasize the need for the speaking partner to <u>keep talking</u> because this pushes the comments beyond the picture and encourages sharing of elements of self.

Use a luggage cart to get the magazines to the classroom. A forklift if class size is large.

Kela Adams
Kinesiology/Health Education
IU Southeast

Generating Discussion From the First Day

It can be difficult to generate student discussion in the classroom, because many students are accustomed to a lecture format. So, I spend considerable time the first day breaking down teacher-student barriers, and giving students a chance to talk. When I enter the classroom, 20-40 bored stares greet me. I begin by introducing myself and the course, and handing out the syllabus. I then ask for questions and usually there are none - the only ones who ask questions are students who have had me as a teacher before.

At this point, most teachers would adjourn the class. Instead, I divide the students into groups of five-seven. In some classes, these groups become permanent collaborative learning groups. I have them count off so they will be in a group will all strangers. Each group selects a spokesperson (someone whose name is nearest the end of the alphabet - this keeps the bossy ones from running the show). The groups are asked to critique the syllabus - to raise questions and concerns, to say what they like and dislike about it.

I tell them I have been known to change the syllabus based on student concerns. And I have.

I tell them I have been known to change the syllabus based on student concerns. And I have. Individuals can feel safe sharing their concerns through the group. Then I give them one or two other tasks, depending on the course. For example, in the family course, they are asked to generate a list of TV shows which could be analyzed for the media assignment described on the syllabus. There is a set amount of time given for this work, usually 20 minutes. I circulate through the room and eavesdrop a little. If a group falls into more than one conversation or off the topic, I gently steer them back on track. After the time is up, I have the students form a big circle with their chairs. The spokesperson introduces the group members to the class, conveys their concerns about the syllabus, and relays any other information asked for. Others are encouraged to chime in, and frequently do.

The classroom immediately becomes very lively as soon as students move into their groups. The class discussion which follows is relaxed and enjoyable. The students are smiling and attentive. They have become familiar with the syllabus at this point, and therefore know exactly what is expected of them in the course. I often fill in additional information, e.g., what I look for in an essay answer. I get a chance to defend topic choices, and grading formats. At the end, the class has become a cohesive group. They are reluctant to leave. The next class will begin with an air of pleasant expectation. We will again sit in a circle and I will lead a structured discussion in which most students will participate.

Linda Haas
Sociology/Women's Studies
Indianapolis

Large Classes

"Students come in, sign up for a learning
group, enjoy refreshments, and meet the
assistant teachers and me."
Mimi Zolan

Dividing a Large Class into Small Discussion Groups

As a teacher of large lecture classes, I have been exploring ways to elicit more student involvement in the learning process as well as vary the subject presentation. A continuing challenge has been class enrollments of about 170 with no discussion sections. I monopolized most of the "air time" during class meetings, along with the small group of students who were bold enough to speak before such a large group. Other students sat back passively either tuning in or tuning out.

This semester I experimented with several exercises that varied the subject presentation, giving students a chance to verbalize about the course material and to learn from each other.

Dividing the class into smaller groups for in-class discussion has worked well, even though my classroom-- a typical lecture hall with fixed seats--is hardly optimal for small group discussions. The architecture has not been a major obstacle and, in some ways, has proved useful. I've used several combinations of small groups: pairs, groups of about five, and dividing the class roughly in half. If you want to have a vigorous discussion where every student speaks, it's probably wise to limit the group size to about five. When my students meet in groups of five, they must leave their seats to face each other. This has not been a problem. Students sit on the steps, the floors, the seats, and some groups go into the adjoining hall. To reduce noise and confusion, it has been helpful to:

1. **Give clear instructions about group formation and the amount of time they are allotted.** E.g., "Turn to the person next to you and..." or "Form a group of half the people in your row (about 5)...." I've used exercises that range from 2 minutes for a paired task, to 15 minutes for a small group discussion, to 45 minutes for a large group discussion.

2. **Give students a specific task.** E.g., "Generate a list of as many..." or "Analyze this case and decide what..." or "Try to reach a unanimous conclusion about...."

3. **Give written as well as oral instructions.** I give each student a sheet of written instructions or write instructions on an overhead.

Jane Mallor
Business Law
IU Bloomington

Teaching Assistants Interacting With Students

Encourage your teaching assistants to interact with the students on your behalf. I ask my teaching assistants to intersperse themselves among the students during class and to interact with them before and after class. This simple strategy contributes greatly to the students' sense that we like them and that we are concerned about them. When I first started teaching large classes, I found my teaching assistants collecting in a small knot at the front of the classroom. Their presence there communicated an unmistakable "us" against "them" message.

When I first started teaching large classes, I found my teaching assistants collecting in a small knot at the front of the classroom.

Once the associate instructors move out into the classroom, up into the balcony, back into the furthest reaches of the auditorium, behavioral problems drop off and student participation increases. Students begin to use the teaching assistants as sources of information and clarification and as conduits for feedback to me.

Bonnie Kendall
Anthropology
IU Bloomington

Debate

Recently, with the class divided roughly in half, we had a debate-style discussion.

☞ I marked the contending sides of the classroom with large signs.

☞ Students were instructed to sit on the side that reflected their position on a controversial case which they had studied and written about.

I gave "traffic control" instructions for the discussion:

☞ They should stand up to signify that they had or wanted the floor.

☞ They should not interrupt each other.

☞ They should keep their remarks brief so others had time to speak.

☞ A student on each side should volunteer to begin the discussion.

☞ I moved to the side, out of the students' line of vision. My absence from the helm seemed to <u>increase</u> the amount of participation, passion, and curiosity.

The quality of student contributions to this discussion was very high.

Also gratifying was that a number of the quieter students who had not spoken before jumped to their feet and eloquently argued their positions.

Afterwards, I reconvened the class for a discussion and/or debriefing. I found the experience generated much more spirited discussions and student involvement than if I had orally presented the same problem during a lecture, then waited for informal student participation.

Jane Mallor
Business Law
IU Bloomington

Mailboxes

Here's a very "nuts and bolts" tip for handling and returning student papers in large lecture classes with no discussion sections:

☞ Each student is given a "mailbox" for his or her graded work. The "mailboxes" are labeled manila folders arranged in alphabetical order for each student, and are kept in a cardboard box (the kind xerox paper comes in).

☞ The boxes are placed on an easily accessible counter in my office reception area. Each time I finish grading a batch of quizzes, exams, or assignments, our clerical staff files them in the students' mailboxes.

☞ Putting a batch of student work in order and filing it is easy because students have been assigned numbers corresponding to the alphabetical order. Students write the number on each piece of work they submit. Putting the work in numerical order is faster and somewhat less tedious than alphabetizing it.

☞ I send an e-mail message to the class distribution list informing them that the work is graded and available for pick up. Students then stop by the office at their convenience without needing to ask anyone for help.

This is working really well in my classes of about 170 students. It saves time for everyone concerned, preserves students' privacy, and keeps an enormous volume of paper in order.

Jane Mallor
Business Law
IU Bloomington

The Book

A Simple Logistical Solution to Office Hours in Large Classes

Each semester, I use a large three-ring binder containing:

Each set of office hours on one page, broken into 15 minute slots.

Listed at the top of each page is the day, date and time of that set of office hours.

The pages are arranged by date and color-keyed.

Each teaching team member is assigned a different color for easy identification.

For instance, in my Introductory Sociology class of 365 students, I regularly have one graduate assistant. My office hours are indicated by the yellow sheets and the graduate assistant's by the blue sheets. We design the office hours to be weekly (each person, say, holding a 2-3 hour set of office hours) but with extra sets clustered around the exams or assignment due dates.

Students may sign up for one or more blocks depending on their perceived needs, and may sign up with other students (e.g., study partners) if they wish. We make it clear in class that we reserve the right to leave early or come late if no one is signed up for slots 24 hours before the office hours start.

During the first two or three class sessions, I explain what "The Book" is, how it works and what our expectations are. After that, I simply mention at the beginning of each class that "The Book" is up front. This has the advantage of reminding students that we take office hours seriously, that we expect them to come, and that they can do so without much hassle. In addition, it has proven very successful in eliminating logistical problems, helping to "crack" the set of initial social-psychological reservations that many students hold about office hours.

Bernice Pescosolido
Institute for Social Research
IU Bloomington

Lecture Outlines

When I first began teaching this class, I simply did not enjoy the atmosphere in the classroom. I wanted an atmosphere where students felt they could ask questions and communicate directly with me, despite the large class size. I was also concerned about the heterogeneous level of preparation by the students. A pace comfortable for some was too fast for others. How could I challenge the better prepared students without losing those less prepared?

I addressed these problems with lecture outlines. These are essentially worksheets, handed out before each lecture, which students fill in during class. This approach has numerous benefits:

Students think during the lecture instead of spending all their time writing. It results in a dramatic difference in the class atmosphere. In a class of 200, students ask questions from the first day, and their questions range from points of clarification to questions that relate the lecture material to information from other courses.

Preparing the outlines helps me prepare better lectures; I'm more organized and forced to distill the material into essential points.

I believe that using the outlines raises the intellectual level of the class. Students can follow complex arguments better if they can listen attentively. I believe students concentrate better.

My approach to teaching this course was adopted by the other course instructor, so I've had the opportunity to see its effectiveness from the students' point of view. I found that the outlines actually make the lectures more interesting and more fun to attend. The worksheet design makes the class time more interactive, and the learning less passive. It's easier to focus on the material, and to think about it.

I think the intuitive reaction to the worksheet idea might be that they make the course "easier." Instead, I find they make it better; they allow students to function as thinkers, not transcribers, and this raises the intellectual level of the class, making it more enjoyable for both students and instructor.

Mimi Zolan
Biology
IU Bloomington

Enlivening Lecture Courses

Asking Questions and Volunteer Recitation Sections

Throughout my teaching career I have frequently been called upon to teach our sophomore-level, introductory course to groups ranging from 160 to 325 students. This environment makes it difficult to inspire students to take an enthusiastic and active role in their education. I have implemented two programs that help offset this hurdle.

First, all students are instructed in a case-briefing process that requires their active conceptualization of each day's material. An integral part of each brief is a section in which each student must ask a minimum of three questions about each case. Students are aware that any time they may be called upon to raise their particular questions in class. Much class time, as well as office hours, are spent refining our ability to ask questions as we encounter the daily reading assignments.

Complementing this program is a volunteer recitation section on each Friday morning. Sessions are optional in that students are given an opportunity to sign up for each Friday's session before the preceding Wednesday. Once a student signs up for a session, he or she must attend. During these recitations, students discuss and debate the concepts explored earlier in the week. Sessions are student-driven in that I try to remain in the background, serving as a catalyst for their own collaborative analysis.

Eric Richards
Business Law
Bloomington

Making a Large Room Feel Small

Teach in a way that makes a large room "feel" small. The size and configuration of most lecture halls tend to inhibit student interactions, which is a major factor in engendering impersonal or alienated attitudes toward the subject matter or toward the class. rude, disruptive and irresponsible student behaviors (talking, sleeping, eating, entering late and exiting early) tend to occur in lecture halls as opposed to smaller classrooms because students in auditoriums perceive themselves as anonymous. On the other hand, a large room can be made to "feel" small if the instructor treats it as if it were.

It is important to circulate about the room before or after classes, talking to the students about how they're doing and answering their questions. Join your teaching assistants in handing out course materials so that you get out among the students and make contact with them. Coming out from behind the podium and moving in the direction of students who ask questions during class has a similarly positive effect. And, of course, nothing gets students involved in a class like collaborative exercises: minute papers that students share with someone sitting next to them, one minute problem solving sessions with neighbors (the noise level in the room will be arresting, but that just shows that people are engaged).

Bonnie Kendall
Anthropology
IU Bloomington

Hold an Open House

I teach half of a genetics lecture course of 200 students. All our students are also enrolled in small collaborative learning groups, which work on weekly problem sets. In these groups, they receive individualized attention plus much practice in problem solving and genetic analysis. So, the basic class format is effective.

However, during the first week of class, I hold "open houses." Students come in during these hours, sign up for a learning group, enjoy refreshments, and meet the assistant teachers and me. This simple plan serves to immediately open communication channels and set the tone for a very interactive semester.

Mimi Zolan
Biology
IU Bloomington

Motivation

Moment of Silence . . .

When discussion classes bog down, most of us have a tendency to try to "fix" things by interjecting our own comments. I've learned just to let the silence continue. Students will soon get used to filling in on their own.

When you ask a class a question and no one responds, try <u>not</u> to ask another question. Make up your mind to count to 60 (one-Mississippi, two-Mississippi, three-Mississippi). You probably won't get past 20-Mississippi before someone will answer.

Silence on the part of students doesn't mean they're wool-gathering, it often means they're thinking about the problem you posed.

Bonnie Kendall
Anthropology
IU Bloomington

Walking Together

The best moments occur when I can alter the learning environment by separating the student from his/her desk and me from the podium. The classroom is education. However, standing side-by-side in the library stacks, sitting across a table in the lounge, walking together around campus, composing jointly at a computer terminal - each of these is learning. I now build at least one such learning environment into each syllabus. My time commitment rises exponentially, but so does my sense of effectiveness.

Robert Otten
English
IU Kokomo

3 X 5 Cards

At the beginning of a class, distribute 3 X 5 cards to the students. Have them write down one or two questions regarding some aspect of the course. Collect the cards and redistribute them. Have students read the question from the card they have just received. This takes the pressure off students who have questions but don't want to appear foolish by asking them.

Variations:

Have students evaluate various aspects of the class (e.g., give a midterm evaluation of the course). Collect the cards and read privately.

Distribute the cards at the end of class for students to write down unanswered questions from that session.

Vince Peterson
Education
IU South Bend

Whips

To begin a class session, a "whip" might be used. Using "whips," <u>each</u> student in succession must respond quickly to an incomplete sentence.

Examples:

"One idea that I learned in the last class session (or from my reading) is...."

"A question that I have about the subject (our class) is...."

"What I would like to see us emphasize today is...."

Important Rules:

The instructor may take notes, but should not respond to any student until the last student has completed the whip. The instructor should also complete the sentence.

Vince Peterson
Education
IU South Bend

Dialogue

The college classroom should be a dialogue between the instructor and <u>all</u> of the students. A quiet class with little student talk is typically a class with little learning, while classes with much student talk focused on live issues are a sign of learning. Thus the challenge that I faced was finding effective strategies to involve all students in our classroom conversations.

I began each semester by requiring that each of my students say something every day. Our classroom activities consist of questions and problems for the students to discuss and discover how to solve, mini-debates, panel discussions, speeches, and small group discussions. During these activities, I make a concerted effort to ensure that we have heard from each student.

Sue Sciame-Giesecke
Speech Communication
IU Kokomo

Power of Voice

While they may understand the importance of a speaker in poetry and drama, students in undergraduate literature classes often are unaware of "voice" in literary narrative. They tend to read texts with their ears closed to the sounds and inflections of human discourse.

To introduce students to the oral pleasures of fiction, I often ask them to participate in class readings. These may include the obvious: giving students "parts" and having them read dialogue (which works well with the vernacular, i.e., Twain, Williams, Marshall). Other students comment on what they have heard, either in brief informal written responses or discussion. Having heard Hemingway dialogue, many students noted for the first time the deadpan power of his monosyllabic language: what had seemed colloquial and "natural" resounded in their ears as mannered and stylized. Conversely, dividing the class into three groups and having them read the three "soliloquies" of Faulkner's <u>The Sound and the Fury</u> simultaneously--an amazing choral effect--convinced them that the novel reflected the chaos of everyday life. Some novels--Doctorow's <u>Ragtime</u>, Morrison's <u>Jazz</u>, Roth's <u>Operation Shylock</u>--ARE oral narratives, verging on the stand-up comic.

Students have great fun "performing" these texts, generating new enthusiasm for reading and quoting from the original, a sense of "ownership" (students tend to remember texts other students have read well), and more interest in interpretation and discussion.

Treating the text as performance is an especially useful technique to introduce literature from other cultures into the classroom. Having students taste the incantorial quality of the Yellow Woman mythologies gives them new ways to understand modern Native American poetry and prose. It also gives the shyer students a way to enter the discourse of a literature class.

Eileen Bender
English
IU South Bend

Entry Tickets

A few years ago, fed up with the "Bermuda Triangle" of the semester (where approximately a third of the class just vanishes during the two or three weeks prior to the semester's end), I started requiring attendance. Since I teach large classes and do not wish to take the time to call the roll, I ask the students for entry tickets -- slips of paper on which they write questions or comments on the readings, ask for clarifications on lectures or suggest topics they'd like to cover in class. The entry tickets count attendance for me and at the same time provide continuous feedback on how the students are doing and how I'm doing with respect to them. No one gets in without an entry ticket. Or, if someone does slip by the ticket-taker empty-handed, his or her attendance isn't counted. Students soon learn to take the exercise seriously.

A few years ago, fed up with the "Bermuda Triangle" of the semester (where approximately a third of the class just vanishes during the two or three weeks prior to the semester's end), I started requiring attendance.

Students may grumble at first about the entry ticket requirement, but if they find that their teacher is willing to answer their questions and respond to their comments, they warm to it. In my classes, participation is up; attendance is up; and completion of reading assignments is up.

The best part about entry tickets is that they generally show such definite progress in the depth and sophistication of students' understanding over the course of the semester that by week five of a course, you can ask students to review their prior entry tickets and most of them will <u>see</u> the evidence of their own intellectual growth and development. They find this very gratifying.

Exit Visas

Like Entry Tickets, Exit Visas serve a double function: they are roll-taking devices as well as chances for students to comment on the class they have just attended, ask for clarification, or draw conclusions and make applications. Exit visas are essentially "minute papers," which can be collected and read, then returned to students with written comments on them.

I alternate Entry Tickets and Exit Visas (the former for Tuesday classes, the latter for Thursday classes), just for the sake of variety.

Bonnie Kendall
Anthropology
IU Bloomington

Spotlighting Student Experts

First and foremost, get to know each of your students personally. Over time, this is actually an easy task. It simply requires your commitment and a willingness to make yourself available to your students when they need you. This implies having a flexible office hours schedule - one that accommodates students rather than the professor.

Questionnaires are unnecessary. Each time a student visits, take a few moments to find out something about that student: where he/she works, type of job/goals and aspirations, family concerns, hobbies, and so forth.

I have found that most students appreciate a genuine concern that the professor may show for them as important people. They will share thoughts quite freely once you have gained their confidence.

I have found that most students appreciate a genuine concern that the professor may show for them as important people. They will share thoughts quite freely once you have gained their confidence. Sooner or later, you will have an opportunity to "spotlight" these students in one of your classes. They appreciate the attention and professional acknowledgement and will land credibility to your instruction.

Occasionally, you will find an "expert" in some subject area. I have frequently asked such experts if they would be willing to give an entire lecture on their area of expertise. I have never had a student decline such a request, nor has one ever given what would be considered a boring presentation. Since most of my students appear to be "sensing" type learners, exposure to practical experiences reenforces their preferred learning style.

Robert Orr
Computer Technology
IUPUI

Supplementing Lectures With Case-Based Learning

I create an implementation/problem solving environment in a lecture course in order to enhance student motivation and participation, and to achieve experiential learning. I do this by implementing case-based learning through:
◊ Custom-designing of knowledge-based expert systems applications for several topics and concepts in a lecture course.
◊ Coupling these to the assignments given to the students so that use of these systems becomes necessary.

Due to its unique design, the expert system is a highly problem-solving oriented environment and its use by students in terms of custom-designed and specifically targeted assignments leads to experiential learning. Students are highly motivated by the interactivity of the methodology employed and the fact that a contemporary information technology is being used as a platform for instruction/learning.

The basic idea behind the undertaking is conversion of information into knowledge through association of such information with specific application/experiences, thus eliminating the "boredom" usually associated with lecture courses by students since no laboratory, problem solving, or design component inherently exists.

Erdogan M. Sener
Construction
IUPUI

There's Nothing Like a Demo

Whenever possible, I use demonstrations in class to illustrate physical principles. Every now and then, disaster strikes! Try this one:

Lay out place settings for two on your table, pour some wine, light the candle...Now to impress your significant other, suddenly pull the tablecloth out from under the dishes. Viola!

This is a demonstration of one of Newton's sacred laws at work, so should never fail - right?
(Moral of the story - don't use your best china.)

Archibald Hendry
Physics
IU Bloomington

Teamwork

In their best-selling book on excellence in corporate management, Peters and Watrman (1982) emphasize the importance of teamwork and information sharing to successful collaborative enterprises. Arguing for "bottom up," or participatory management styles, as opposed to those that are "top down" or autocratic, they propose that the best manager - the wisest and most successful - attend most closely to the people in their organizations "out on the front lines" and "down in the trenches." They listen to their suggestions; they value their feedback.

If Peters and Waterman's insights are extendable at all to academia, then Associate Instructors or Teaching Assistants must be taken seriously as members of the teaching profession - not treated as the professor's handmaidens. Every effort should be made to solicit their points of view on planning and implementation of the course, even though the professor must ultimately take responsibility for deciding what he or she is going to do.

I have discovered three indisputable facts about teaching assistants:

They hate being used.

They hate being ignored.

They hate being uninformed.

From this it seems to follow that professors should:

Avoid giving teaching assistant assignments that they don't at least try to participate in themselves (e.g., making up or grading exams).

Solicit their assistants' thoughts and opinions about how the course is going and how it can be improved.

Keep their assistants current on their plans for the course.

Weekly staff meetings are essential in this regard; furthermore, monthly information-sharing meetings between the teaching staff and interested student representatives from the class are genuinely helpful.

Bonnie Kendall
Anthropology
IU Bloomington

EVALUATION

Continuous Assessment

In lecture classes, especially in large freshman lectures, it is particularly helpful to stop talking at the end of every testable unit and give a mini-quiz, i.e. present a few multiple choice questions over the material just covered. The individual student's task is to select an answer and then jot down a few sentences explaining why the answer chosen is better than the next best alternative. Pairs or trios of students can then compare their answers and try to clarify reasons for discrepancies. The next step is to survey the class to determine which answers were selected and why those alternatives were favored. This device allows many kinds of misunderstandings and naive appreciations to be brought to light and corrected before they become established in the students' minds. It helps teachers understand their students' reasoning processes so that they know what needs to be taught differently and what needs to be retaught.

It is particularly helpful to stop talking at the end of every testable unit and give a mini-quiz . . . the student is getting feedback on his or her level of performance before taking an examination that counts toward a grade.

Short answer questions work just as well as multiple choice questions in most cases. A third alternative is to show a transparency illustrating the information just covered and have the students write briefly on their understanding of it.

In any of these circumstances, the student is getting feedback on his or her level of performance, as well as on your expectations, before he or she has to take an examination that counts toward the grade in the course.

Craig Nelson
Biology
IU Bloomington

Peer Evaluations

One of my courses involves extensive peer evaluations of writing. Because we deal with controversial issues as well as personal writing style, I need an atmosphere where criticism is both constructive and hard-nosed. Obviously, I try to exemplify that balance in my own evaluations of their work. But I've found the real problem is giving students the freedom to be critical without taking personal offense.

I've found the real problem is giving students the freedom to be critical without taking personal offense.

To do that, I've adopted two strategies. First, I give students a piece of writing to criticize in class. Although I don't identify it, the writing is my own. It's also terrible: vague, undocumented, bloated with metaphors run amok. After they have had a chance to rip it apart, I find a way to let them know it is mine. I tell them how proud I was of that piece the day I wrote it. The messages are clear. If the instructor can take it in good humor, so can anyone else. And what we see as great writing may need some improvement after all.

Second, I organize the class into small groups of six. These groups - the place where the peer evaluation goes on - stay the same all semester. **The students get to know each other well. They feel more comfortable criticizing the writing and arguments of other group members. And they feel the constraint of friendship which ensures that criticism is constructive.** As a result, the evaluations are always lively; but only once in three years has a session gotten tense. And the student deserved it.

Dave Boeyink
Journalism
IU Bloomington

Grade Books

In classes where I grade students by their participation or by their improvement, I find the standard grade book inadequate. This is because in general grade books are designed only for recording test and quiz score information.

I use a composition notebook instead. I put each student's name at the top of a different page, recording such things as notes, impressions, summaries of conferences, quality of contributions to class, and times and dates of all interactions. I share these pages with students so that they are aware that records are being kept and can discuss my impressions of their performances.

When it is time to assess the student's performance at the end of the semester, I have records for students that include both quantitative and qualitative data concerning them: test scores, attendance record, and notes on their intellectual growth through the semester.

Janet Streepey
Honors Program
IU Bloomington

Teaching Journal

Keep a class notebook. After each class record where you stopped, what questions were on the floor at the time and who posed them, what you hope to guide the class toward in the next meeting, plus important contributions to the class and who made them. Write down which explanations worked and which failed. Note student-generated examples linking course materials to the contexts of their lives, especially those with which you yourself are unfamiliar (those related to their peer culture: music they listen to, television shows they watch, books they read and so forth).

This record-keeping takes less than five minutes if done right after class, but lends real continuity and integrity to the class. It helps you avoid teaching the same material again during the week (unless that is your deliberate aim), which is particularly valuable if you're teaching multiple sections of the same course.

Such a teaching journal is invaluable for managing subsequent repetitions of the course in other semesters.

Janet Streepey
Honors Program
IU Bloomington

Write Yourself A Letter

In courses such as Personal Health, I find it useful to close the semester by having each student write a letter to her or himself discussing specific plans for behavioral and attitudinal changes she or he will make in light of new knowledge and skills developed throughout the semester. I provide the paper and an envelope which they self-address to the residence they expect to be in three months hence. I ask students to describe in some detail the kinds of health encouraging, improving, preserving steps that they will make in those ensuing three months.

Students write their letters, seal them themselves and give them to me so that I can mail the confidential letters three months after the class ends. The letters serve as reminders and reinforcers of various health-related "resolutions" that students make throughout the semester. I note the appropriate mailing date on my calendar and despatch them as promised to students.

Kela Adams
Education/Physical Education
IU Southeast

Midterm Feedback

Most instructors use the end of the semester evaluation forms to obtain feedback on their courses. One problem with this procedure is that if something could have been done during the semester to improve the course, it's then too late. Some instructors use a variety of mid-term course evaluations which allow them to make "course corrections" and enhance student learning in the second half of the course. These approaches include:

1. A one page open-ended evaluation form which can include questions such as:

   A. What have been some of the strong features of this class to date?

   B. What aspects of this class would you like to see strengthened or changed? How would you suggest making these changes?

   C Are there any mannerisms/behaviors of the instructor that you would like to see changed?

   D. Other comments, praises, and suggestions.

2. Have students give anonymous, unstructured responses on a 3 X 5 card to an open-ended question(s) about the course instruction.

3. Have two or three students volunteer to collect and summarize class data from either of the above methods, then meet with the instructor after class to discuss results to make sure criticisms and suggestions are not misconstrued.

Kela Adams
Education
IU Southeast

Keepers

Getting students (or workshop participants) to take a deeply rooted ownership of the learning process is an ongoing challenge. Too often they overlook that learning is something that happens within the LEARNER rather than is caused by the teacher. In my view, the most the teacher has to do with the process is to support, assist, abet, inspire and hope to influence the learner in ways that make her or his learning easier.

A technique I've used effectively is a "Keepers" Sheet (example on next page) that students use to note their key ideas, insights, and discoveries drawn from a given class. Here's how it works: at the end of an instructional unit, after the test or summative evaluation of whatever kind, distribute a "Keepers" Sheet to each student and ask that she or he record the valuable or important notions they most want to permanently "own" or incorporate into their knowledge or skills base.

The "Keepers" Sheet can, of course, be a page from the student's own notebook. It seems to me, however, that it is more effective to present a special form for the students' use in developing their document. Encourage students to refer to their "Keepers" over time after the course ends to reinforce their thinking, and serve as a basis for development of new insights along the way.

Kela Adams
Education
IU Southeast

KEEPERS

Ideas I discovered, want to remember, act upon, or pursue further

Spring, 1993

1. Most health problems - my behavior, choices are powerful influences.

2. Don't try to "cheer up" or "cut off" a friend who is talking suicide - encourage to talk and get them to professional help...STAT!

3. Apples, oranges, bananas = FAST FOOD!

4. Exercises - start slowly and taper off so I won't get hurt.

5. Don't blame people with AIDS.

6. Self-Knowledge is basis for successful relationships.

7. Too much alcohol - reduces me to level of subhuman intelligence.

8. Death/an option (I'm not invulnerable or immune.).

9. It is NOT selfish to consider my own needs.

10. Exhaustion and wellbeing are mutually exclusive.

_____   _____

Signature   Date

Final Feedback

One of the most common instructional behaviors that is hardest to justify professionally is giving a final exam and then assigning a final grade based on the results of the exam without giving the students specific feedback on the results. Ethically, this seems to be a very questionable practice. Without corrective feedback, students may believe their erroneous ideas are correct!

One way that I handle this is to give the actual test back to the students indicating where their errors are. I then place a set of correct answers on reserve in the library so that comparisons can be made. In the case of essay tests, I place one or two full-value answers for each essay question. These "correct answers" may be those which were prepared in advance and used to help grade essay items consistently, or I may use copies of student responses that received full credit. Having students attain full and accurate closure on their course learning is of far greater value than protecting the "sanctity" of a few test questions. This practice does force the instructor to have a large reservoir of good test items so that the same items are not used each semester.

Without corrective feedback, students may believe their erroneous ideas are correct!

Another option is to arrange for an optional feedback session after grades have been submitted. At this session, test results can be discussed fully. Test papers can be closely monitored and collected at the end of the session. This approach is most desirable because it allows discussion of the content in each test item, which corrects and strengthens learning. It should be stressed at the beginning of a feedback session that its purpose is to clarify ideas and to assure that facts are accurate, not to "negotiate" a few extra points credit.

Vince Peterson
Education
IU South Bend

Changing Behavior

In the Personal Health H363 course, I definitely hold out hope of changing behavior and having students adopt more healthful lifestyles. Two techniques seem to help:

During the first class meeting, I distribute "preowned" (used) manila folders to students asking them to create a name card for their desk that depicts attainable and valued health improvement/sustaining goals that they might expect to accomplish before the end of the semester. Half of the folder rests on the writing surface and the other half hangs down in front for all to see. In addition to the student's first name, the "display surface" of the folder illustrates or suggests behavioral changes that the individual intends to adopt during the semester. Illustrations can take the form of drawings, artful or otherwise, collage or bas relief! Dietary changes, improved interpersonal communication, increased exercise and more rest, reduced alcohol use, and more constructive approaches to dealing with emotions.

At the last class meeting, students discuss their progress during the semester in adopting a healthy lifestyle.

Then, I give students a piece of writing paper and an envelope, asking them to write THEMSELVES a letter encouraging still more progress, setting more goals, and applauding successes already realized. Students are asked to self-address the envelopes, seal their letters within (signed "with love," of course) and return the letters to me so that I can mail them to each student in three months.

Many students have told me they are pleasantly surprised by the subsequent arrival of this confidential letter which they'd forgotten they'd written and find its contents a useful reinforcement and a valuable reminder to continue (or begin to) focus on self-care issues.

Kela Adams
Education
IU Southeast

Self-Assessment

My friend was dashing out of a local deli, a look of worry on her face. She was on her way to meet with a junior colleague who was struggling in a bid for tenure, she told me. As chair of her unit, she was dreading what she knew she would have to tell her.

Why don't you ask her instead how she herself thinks she's doing? I asked. Ask her what she thinks she's doing well, and what she thinks needs improvement. Then ask her what she thinks she needs to do if she is to earn tenure, and what you might do to help her. That way you probably won't have to deliver all the bad news yourself. And if she's right about how she's doing, you can reward her for her insights. If she's not right, at least you know where she's coming from. She might also tell you some things you hadn't thought about. And you can be there for her, to offer her your help.

My friend look surprised, then relieved, then grateful.

Have you ever thought of becoming a department chair? she asked.

I was flattered. But the truth is, there was nothing especially original or profound about my advice. It was simply something that I have discovered works - in my teaching, in informal interactions with students of writing, and occasionally even with my children. It is the simple art of self-assessment. And since I began routinely to use it in my teaching, it has made me a much happier and more effective teacher.

Self-assessment, as I have used it in writing classes, works like this:

☺ After each assignment, students write down their "gut reactions" to what they have written.

☺ Then they write what they believe to be the focus or message of their paper, their evaluation of the supporting information, the organization, and the writing. What do they like? What do they think could be improved? What improvements did they make in this work over previous work?

☺ Also, what do they want me to help them with on the next assignment or the rewrite (if there is one)?

☺ Is there anything else they want me to know? Almost without exception, students tell me things that are invaluable to my own assessments. They point out improvements I might not have noticed. Often students know precisely where the problems lie, and even what to do about them. Sometimes students even point up weaknesses I might not have noticed, but which provide the keys to improvement. Importantly, self-assessments also help make the classroom less adversarial and therefore a more satisfying place for students and teachers alike.

As for my friend, the department chair, she tells me the meeting with her junior colleague went much better than she had expected.

Not everything was ironed out in the session, but the junior faculty member left the meeting feeling supported. My friend left the meeting feeling appreciated.

Was I surprised? Not at all. If my students have taught me anything, it is that people often are enormously wise if we allow them to be.

Holly Stocking
Journalism
IU Bloomington

Student Self-Evaluation

I have initiated a process of student self-evaluation in each of my upper-level courses. Three times each semester, students are required to do a detailed evaluation of all aspects of their performance in the course based upon a self-evaluation sheet which I provide (sample on next page). In the final evaluation, they assign themselves a grade based on their assessment and this contributes 10% or 15% of their final grade. I have rarely found that my own evaluation and the students' are more than a grade level apart, and students tend to assign themselves grades lower than mine about as often as higher. The sample shown can easily be modified to serve any course.

Mike Keen
Sociology
IU South Bend

S319 Sociology of Science
Self-Evaluation Guide

PLEASE use this sheet as a guide for the self-evaluation of your performance in the class. This evaluation should be written in the form of an essay and discuss each aspect of your performance as outlined below:

A. Readings:

Which did you do	Thoroughly	Mostly	So So	Never Got To
1. Bacon	____	____	____	____
2. Mendelssohn	____	____	____	____
3. Zilsel	____	____	____	____
4. Merton	____	____	____	____
5. Van den Daele	____	____	____	____
6. Kuhn	____	____	____	____
7. Merchant	____	____	____	____
8. Mulkay	____	____	____	____
9. Bloor	____	____	____	____
10. Bernstein	____	____	____	____
11. Horkheimer	____	____	____	____

B. Class Participation:

1. How many classes did you miss? _____

2. Was your participation qualitatively <u>Strong</u> <u>Good</u> <u>Adequate</u> <u>Minimal</u>?

    a. Include in this discussion an evaluation of those occasions in which you lead a discussion or summarized a reading.

3. What are your strengths and weaknesses in the oral realm?

C. Assignments:

Evaluate each of the written assignments in terms of: preparation/research and written product (content, clarity, creativity, style, etc.).

    1. Journal
    2. Exams
    3. Book Review

D. What have you learned by being in this class in the area of skills; in the area of knowledge?

E. Are there any other comments you wish to make?

F. What grade do you give yourself for your work in this class? _____

HOW GOOD A MOTIVATOR ARE YOU?

Check your motivational practices by rating yourself on the questions below. Add your totals in each column. Score yourself as follows: 90-100, excellent; 80-90, good; 70-80, fair; 10-poor.

	Usually (4 points)	Sometimes (2 points)	Never (0 points)
1. I believe my students are competent and trustworthy.	_____	_____	_____
2. I avoid labeling students.	_____	_____	_____
3. I avoid sarcasm, put-downs, and ridicule of students.	_____	_____	_____
4. I send explicit invitations to succeed.	_____	_____	_____
5. I listen to what my students really say.	_____	_____	_____
6. I let my students know they are missed.	_____	_____	_____
7. I make good use of student experts in the class.	_____	_____	_____
8. I use heterogeneous groups to build interdependence.	_____	_____	_____
9. I teach leadership and communicate skills.	_____	_____	_____
10. I avoid overemphasis on competition, reward, and winning.	_____	_____	_____
11. I help groups evaluate their effectiveness in group process.	_____	_____	_____
12. I give equal time, attention, and support to low-ability students.	_____	_____	_____
13. I communicate high expectations to my students.	_____	_____	_____
14. I focus on future success rather than past failures.	_____	_____	_____
15. I look for what is positive in student work and behavior.	_____	_____	_____
16. I set and communicate clear goals for behavior.	_____	_____	_____

	Usually (4 points)	Sometimes (2 points)	Never (0 points)
17. I use well-designed, thought-provoking questions to stimulate readiness.	_____	_____	_____
18. I use objects as "focusing events" to stimulate interest.	_____	_____	_____
19. I use brainstorming to stimulate interest before beginning a lesson.	_____	_____	_____
20. I use set induction activities that connect a present experience to a lesson concept.	_____	_____	_____
21. I ask low-risk, open-ended questions.	_____	_____	_____
22. I wait three to five seconds after asking a divergent question.	_____	_____	_____
23. I suspend judgment and redirect a question to get multiple responses.	_____	_____	_____
24. I paraphrase and clarify responses instead of judging and praising.	_____	_____	_____
25. I personalize learning.	_____	_____	_____

Erwin Boschmann
Faculty Development
IUPUI
Reprinted with permission

Collaborative Activities with Research Reports in Elementary Education

The teaching challenge that I encountered in the course E590, Research in Education, was helping graduate students become users and evaluators of research reports in elementary education. Consequently, I employed a project developed at Michigan State University titled "Helping Teachers Use Research Findings: the Consumer-Validation Process."

The purpose of the project was to provide graduate students with a body of research on a specified topic and to direct them to design and use learning activities in their classrooms. After they introduced the activities, the students were asked to determine if the results from the learning experience validated or invalidated the research.

I selected the topic "Cooperative Learning in the Elementary School" to teach the Consumer-Validation Process. After I shared research on the effectiveness of cooperative learning and techniques for employing the research, I asked the students in my class to design and conduct several cooperative learning activities in their classrooms on an assigned curricular area such as reading, mathematics, science, etc.

Each activity was evaluated by the student to determine its effectiveness. Those activities which validated the research on cooperative learning were saved; those that didn't were discarded. Each of the ten times that the project was conducted, the consumers (students) were able to identify several activities which validated research on cooperative learning.

The consumers (students) have developed ten activity booklets of research-validated activities employing the cooperative learning strategy. The booklets are comprised of cooperative learning activities for teaching social studies, science, reading, mathematics, and writing.

Lowell Madden
Education
IP Ft. Wayne

Using Negatives to Teach Counterpoint

T531 is a counterpoint course in which students become intimate with Bach's style by studying his music and writing pieces in his style. Students study scores and lists of appropriate features to include and pitfalls to avoid, but they still have trouble evaluating their own writing, spotting their own errors.

Tactic:

In class, pass out examples with lots of errors. Pair students up and assign each pair a specific portion to look at, discuss, and report to the class in about 10 minutes. It seems to be easier to criticize some anonymous bad counterpoint than to evaluate one's own work. In addition, different students focus on different stylistic features, so during the discussion they learn how their partners think when writing/evaluating counterpoint. They implicitly share their compositional strategies and priorities with their partners.

Gary Potter
Music Theory
IU Bloomington

33

Readiness Profile

Just as a speaker inquires ahead of time about his audience, so a teacher wants to know about his class. One of the first questions a teacher has about a new class concerns the preparedness of the students. Are they ready for this class? What will permit them to succeed; what might cause failure? How must I, the teacher, adjust to meet the student's level?

Previous performance is often checked and used as a guide to predict future performance. Grades and reports from previous work and comments from previous teachers are possible guides. Because algebra and mathematics are so basic to all science courses, we have often used performance in these fields as indicative of likely success in, say chemistry. However, often we found this, by itself, to be an unreliable indicator. Many personal variables are as important as mental dexterity.

Many personal variables are as important as mental dexterity.

Counseling thousands of students has made it clear that mathematical thinking ability is but one facet of student life that will measure performance. After much thought and inquiry, it became clear that there really are four areas contributing to success or failure in a student's performance.

The first of these is the student's educational background. Proper previous training is a must for many courses. The rigor of studying mathematics or foreign languages trains the mind to be flexible.

A second area is that of the student's personal affairs. If the home life is in disarray, there just is not much of a chance for successful studies. The number of hours on a job, the habits of entertainment, family obligations - all influence studies.

The next indicator is self-motivation. One's outlook on life, attitude, extent of self-discipline, and perceived reason for studying - all say something about how one will approach studying.

Finally, the maturity of the thinking level is important. If the student continues to operate strictly on the concrete level and is virtually unable to reason in abstract terms, there very likely will be upcoming problems.

Given the above truths, I have developed a set of forty questions, ten in each of the four areas, to gauge the readiness of my students. Table 5.1 gives the currently used items. The Educational Background is measured in questions 1, 2, 3, 13, 14, 21, 22, 29, 33, and 37. Personal Affairs are tested in questions 4, 7, 10, 15, 18, 23, 26, 30, 34, and 38; whereas the level of Motivation is looked for in questions 5, 8, 11, 16, 19, 24, 27, 31, 35, and 40. Finally, an attempt is made to understand the student's Thinking Level through questions 6, 9, 12, 17, 20, 25, 28, 32, 36, and 39.

The students are given this questionnaire soon after the second week of the term, with the announcement that "this is not a test or quiz, but rather a counseling tool meant to help us help you." The answer sheet is simple and easy, providing plenty of space for scratch work. Twenty minutes working time is allowed.

Four sets of keys are prepared, one for each of the areas being tested. Some questions may have numerous acceptable answers, others may have only one true or acceptable answer. Thus, we find question 2 acceptable for our course if b, c, d, or e are checked; however, in question 37 only b is true. The number of acceptable answers out of ten is counted; and the result drawn as an arrow on the appropriate gauge, as shown in Figure 5.2. The overall readiness is simply a composite of the four areas.

While this tool is an interesting and powerful predictor of grade, it should be used strictly as a counseling tool. It can be considered valid only at the time it was taken. It may remain valid if nothing in the student's life changes, and it becomes invalid as soon as something does change.

A quick glance at the Readiness Profile tells me where I can make suggestions to the student without having to ask forty questions. If the Educational Background gauge shows a low reading, I may suggest reviews, or other coursework; if Personal Affairs is low, I may suggest reducing the hours on the job or the course load, or I may not be able to change much, but at least I can be understanding; if Motivation is low, I have a challenge on my hands; and finally if the Thinking Level is low it may mean that the student operates on the concrete and must be helped through examples, graphs, and diagrams.

Table 5.1 C 101 Readiness Profile

This questionnaire is meant to help us help you. It is therefore important that you answer all questions in complete honesty. Don't try to "psych out" the answers. All results will be held in strictest confidence.

- Be sure you answer *all* questions.
- Pick only *one* answer to each question.
- Answer by *filling* in the circles on the separate ANSWER SHEET.

1. How much math did you take in high school?

   a. none
   b. 1 class
   c. 2 classes
   d. 3 classes
   e. 4 or more classes

2. How much college math have you taken or are you now taking?

   a. none
   b. 1 class
   c. 2 classes
   d. 3 classes
   e. 4 or more classes

3. On the average your math grades generally were about

   a. does not apply-
      never taken
   b. C or less
   c. B
   d. A

4. About how many hours per week do you spend on the job?

   a. I have no job
   b. 14 hours or less
   c. 15 to 19 hours
   c. 15 to 19 hours
   d. 20 to 24 hours
   e. 25 or more hours

5. On a scale of *a* to *e* define your general attitude:

   depressed   positive
   unsure   confident
   dragging   eager

   a   b   c   d   e

6. Think of a ball of clay with a certain volume. The ball is now rolled into a sausage shape. The volume of the sausage shape is

   a. the larger
   b. the smaller
   c. the same
   d. depends on the length

7. When do you usually study?

   a. early morning
   b. between classes
   c. after work
   d. evenings
   e. weekends

8. Which statement do you agree with most? Life is . . .

   a. a series of obstacles
   b. a lot of work
   c. a big challenge
   d. an exciting venture

9. You are in the grocery store to buy Pork and Beans. Brand A offers a 32-oz. can for .89, while brand B offers three 15-oz. cans for $1.29. Which is the cheaper buy?

   a. brand A
   b. brand B
   c. both cost the same

10. As far as your college work is concerned, do you receive support and encouragement from home?

    a. yes
    b. no

11. On a scale of *a* to *e* define your level of self-discipline.

    no self-   very self-
    discipline   disciplined

    a   b   c   d   e

12. Insert the missing number in the sequence: 2 5 8 11 _?_

    a. 12
    b. 13
    c. 14
    d. 15

13. Of the subjects chemistry, physics, astronomy, and geology, how many semesters total have you taken (include high school and college)?

    a. none
    b. 1
    c. 2
    d. 3
    e. 4 or more

14. Your average grade in the above subjects usually was about

    a. does not apply-
       never taken
    b. C or less
    c. B
    d. A

15. Are you responsible for children or other members of your household?

    a. yes   b. no

16. In the last year or so, how many books have you read which are not related to class work?

    a. none   c. 2 to 3   e. 6 or more
    b. one   d. 4 to 5

17. Insert the number missing from the brackets:

    347   (418)   489
    643   (   )   721

    a. 650   c. 702
    b. 682   d. 714

18. Where do you study most of the time

    a. table in my room
    b. on the bed
    c. dining room or kitchen
    d. library

19. While studying, most of my time is devoted to

    a. reviewing notes   c. reading
    b. outlining   d. rewriting
                          e. doing problems

20. Consider the following four animals and four names: cat, dog, goat, horse; Angel, Beauty, King, Rover. Which name goes with which animal? You know that
    -King is smaller than dog or Rover
    -horse is younger than Angel
    -Beauty is oldest and is good friend of dog
    Match the correct animal with its name.

    a. the goat's name is Beauty
    b. the dog's name is Rover
    c. the horse's name is King
    d. the cat's name is Angel

21. How many semesters of foreign languages have you taken (include high school and college)?

    a. none   c. 2   e. 4 or more
    b. 1   d. 3

22. Your average grade generally received in foreign languages was about

    a. does not apply-   c. B
       never taken   d. A
    b. C or less

23. Do you have to work in order to be able to go to school?

    a. yes   b. no

24. Think about your study pattern and answer one of the following
    I study . . .

    a. some
    b. whenever there is time
    c. a lot before exams
    d. on a set schedule

25. Enterprise: tripe, peer, rite, rent, print, pair, rips. Which is the odd-man-out?

    a. tripe   c. print
    b. rite   d. pair
                     e. rips

26. Think about your leisure time. About how much time per week is devoted to socializing, dating, TV, movies, play, etc.?

    a. 4 hours or less
    b. 5-6 hours
    c. 7-9 hours
    d. 10-12 hours
    e. 13 or more hours

27. Why are you in college? (Choose one):

    a. parent encouragement
    b. employer encouragement
    c. need credits for a degree
    d. I want to

36

28. Which does not belong:
    New York, London, Paris, Tokyo

    a. New York   c. Paris
    b. London   d. Tokyo

29. How much studying did you do in high school?

    a. less than 5 hours/week
    b. 5-9 hours/week
    c. 10-14 hours/week
    d. 15 or more hours/week

30. On a scale of *a* to *e* describe your relationship
    with those with whom you live.

    stressful   happy
    anxious   harmonious
    impossible   peaceful

    a   b   c   d   e

31. Do you have definite, detailed goals which are
    checked periodically?

    a. yes   b. no

32. A 250-g rock is crushed and treated to remove
    all the iron. After all the iron is taken out the
    rock residue weighs 200 grams. What is the
    percent of iron?

    a. 12.5%   c. 25.0%
    b. 20.0%   d. 80.0%

33. Your GPA (based on 4.0 = perfect) is closest to

    a. 2   c. 3   e. 4
    b. 2.5   d. 3.5

34. How many credit hours are you taking?

    a. less than 6   c. 12-15
    b. 6-11   d. 16 or more

35. What are your true feelings about taking
    chemistry?

    a. would never take it if I didn't have to
    b. would prefer taking something else
    c. it may be tough going, but I'm ready to make
       a go of it
    d. it is a challenging adventure
    e. I chose to take it

36. It is possible to predict temperature by adding 40
    to the number of chirps the snowy tree cricket
    produces in 15 seconds. What is the temperature
    if a chirp count was 120 per minute?

    a. 30   c. 70
    b. 55   d. 80

37. Given: $3 - x = 5$, what is x?

    a. -3   c. 0
    b. -2   d. 3
                     e. 5

38. In your opinion, do you eat, drink, smoke, or
    sleep too much?

    a. yes   b. no

39. A box contains 18 donuts. At first sampling a
    third of them is eaten. An hour later, a third of
    the remainder is eaten. how many donuts are
    left?

    a. 4   c. 8
    b. 6   d. 12

Time	Mon.	Tues.	Wed.	Thurs.	Fri.	Sat.	Sun.
6-7 am							
7-8 am							
5-9 pm							
9-10 pm							
10-11 pm							
11-12 pm							
12-6 am							

40. Based on the above schedule, what is your study
    time for chemistry?

    a. up to 5 hours per week
    b. 6 to 10 hours
    c. 11 to 14 hours
    d. 15 hours or more

Your Name_____

_____

Name _____

Section _____

ANSWER SHEET

	a b c d e		a b c d e		a b c d e		a b c d e
1.	0 0 0 0 0	11.	0 0 0 0 0	21.	0 0 0 0 0	31.	0 0 0 0 0
2.	0 0 0 0 0	12.	0 0 0 0 0	22.	0 0 0 0 0	32.	0 0 0 0 0
3.	0 0 0 0 0	13.	0 0 0 0 0	23.	0 0 0 0 0	33.	0 0 0 0 0
4.	0 0 0 0 0	14.	0 0 0 0 0	24.	0 0 0 0 0	34.	0 0 0 0 0
5.	0 0 0 0 0	15.	0 0 0 0 0	25.	0 0 0 0 0	35.	0 0 0 0 0
6.	0 0 0 0 0	16.	0 0 0 0 0	26.	0 0 0 0 0	36.	0 0 0 0 0
7.	0 0 0 0 0	17.	0 0 0 0 0	27.	0 0 0 0 0	37.	0 0 0 0 0
8.	0 0 0 0 0	18.	0 0 0 0 0	28.	0 0 0 0 0	38.	0 0 0 0 0
9.	0 0 0 0 0	19.	0 0 0 0 0	29.	0 0 0 0 0	39.	0 0 0 0 0
10.	0 0 0 0 0	20.	0 0 0 0 0	30.	0 0 0 0 0	40.	0 0 0 0 0

Answer Key

	Personal Affairs	Motivation	Thinking Level
Educational Background			
	4. a, b	5. d. e	6. c
1. d, e	7. a, d, e	8. c, d	9. a
2. b, c ,d, e	10. a	11. d, e	12. c
3. c, d	15. b	16. c, d, e	17. b
13. d, e	18. a, d	19. e	20. a
14. c, d	23. b	24. d	25. d
21. c, d, e	26. a, b, c	27. d	28. a
22. c, d	30. d, e	31. a	32. b
29. c, d	34. a, b, c	35. c, d, e	36. c
33. c, d, e	38. b	40. c, d	39 c
37. b			

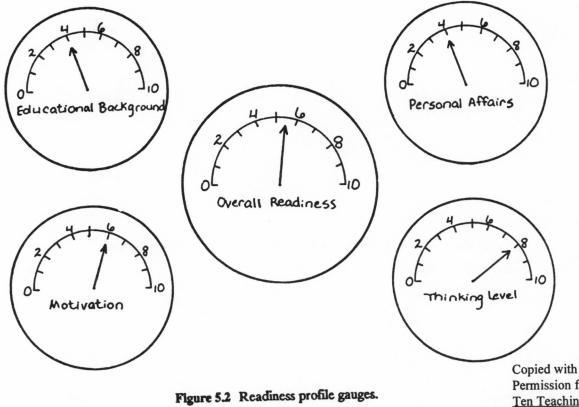

Figure 5.2 Readiness profile gauges.

Copied with
Permission from
<u>Ten Teaching Tools</u>
Ten Secrets to Total
Teaching Success by
Erwin Boschmann
IUPUI
Kendall/Hunt
Publishing Co.
Dubuque, Iowa

CRITICAL THINKING

". . . a war is not over when the last shot is fired."
Clifford Scott

Work Groups: Promoting Real Life Experience

Forming a unified work team to obtain a set goal is one of the most difficult challenges facing students in the marketing program. I help students achieve this by having them participate in the **"Leonard J. Raymond Collegiate Echo Competition."** This competition promotes thinking in real-life business terms and prepares them to compete for future scholarships and prizes.

The competition requires that students have a basic outline of a real company such as HBO/Cinemax (1992) or American Express (1993). With this information, students work in groups of four, whose main goal is to brainstorm an advertising campaign. Brainstorming consists of everything from the initial idea through the actual implementation of the full campaign.

Students are given the entire semester to work on their project with checkpoint deadlines throughout the semester. This is combined with the regular course textbooks and all supplemental material relevant to the course work.

Free to choose their ideas and design their campaigns, groups learn:

✌ The real life situation of compromise.

✌ To evaluate other group members.

✌ To accept both positive and negative evaluation results.

Participating in this competition teaches that cooperation and willingness to compromise are two situations which professionals in any field must contend with.

Monle Lee
Marketing
IU South Bend

Practicality and Imagination

Theatre Design requires a unique combination of practicality and imagination. I often find that my students have either one or the other, but rarely both. Each semester is a challenge to bring out the necessary combination for successful projects. I've had the most success with a two-week hands-on project.

Although each student must complete his/her own project, the entire class is encouraged to work together on a contour flat.

✌I demonstrate each of the five steps in the project. Then the students plunge in and I step to the sidelines.

✌The project is calculated to require practical skills <u>and</u> imagination to complete.

✌Without a teacher "leading," the students soon demonstrate their strengths while looking around for someone whose strengths complement their own. Teams invariably form and reform during the two-week period as the steps are completed.

✌Because each person must turn in his/her <u>own</u> project, the tendency for one person to "do it all" that sometimes occurs in group projects is avoided. Students feel less shy about getting help from each other than from the instructor, and are often pleasantly surprised when <u>their</u> help is sought.

Susan VanDyke
Theatre Design
IU Southeast

Concept Teams

Part of introductory sociology includes the requirement that students become familiar with various descriptive conceptual typologies (or "ideal types"). Lectures are an "efficient" means for presenting such typologies; however, they can also be very dull, encouraging rote memorization without helping students develop an understanding of underlying principles and the ability to apply them. An alternative approach is to divide classes into groups of two or three students called, "Concept Teams." Each team categorizes a series of examples into two or three conceptual typologies.

To illustrate, I use this technique to clarify the meaning and application of "social groups," "aggregates," and "categories." I introduce the project with an overview of how sociological analysis often begins by systematically conceptualizing various features of social reality into descriptive "ideal types." I then explain the general nature of the activity and assign students to several "Concept Teams." Next, I place the following diagram on the board:

features of "social groups" (regular interaction, identifiable structure, consensus on values and goals, shared identity), to illustrate the largely happenstance qualities of groups comprising "aggregates," and to show how shared, common features (not interaction) define groups considered as "categories."

The activity concludes with a discussion of how knowing the criteria underlying the application of "ideal types" helps us understand and apply the concepts to real world examples and how to deal with ambiguous cases.

Equally important, it engages students and makes them active learners rather than passive note-takers. It also helps create informal ties among students and sometimes leads to learning activities outside the classroom such as informal study groups.

Earl Wysong
Sociology
IU Kokomo

SOCIAL GROUPS	AGGREGATES	CATEGORIES

Alongside the diagram I list several examples and ask each team to complete two specific tasks:

1. Assign each sample to one of the three columns.

2. Develop a rationale or explanation for their choices. The list of examples includes (e.g.): teenagers, bowling team, crowd at an accident, Elvis fans, high school clique, passengers on an airline flight, physicians, this sociology class, college juniors, UFO enthusiasts, shoppers at a mall, MTV viewers, retirees.

After the teams develop their selections and explanations, the class votes on which of the three columns each example should fit into, and I list the results on the board. A discussion of the pros and cons of the class votes leads to a consideration of the criteria that guided the teams' application of the typologies. I use the discussion to clarify four key

Strong Contrasts/
Dialogic Thinking

Have you ever taken an art history class where the teacher presented two color slides simultaneously while lecturing on the similarities and differences between the works of art depicted? The "two slide technique," frankly copied from art historians, has become my favorite device for stimulating discussion in undergraduate anthropology classes; it should work equally well for any number of other disciplines. Here's an example:

I present pictures of two funerals: John F. Kennedy's and the Ayatolla Khomeni's. I ask students to draw a vertical line down the center of a piece of paper. Describing what they see on the left slide, they jot down words that come to mind on the left side of the vertical line, then repeat the process on the right side for the right slide. They have approximately one minute to do this. Afterwards, they compare their lists to others' lists around them. I ask them to volunteer common words, which I record for the class with an overhead projector. I ask them to compare the tone of the words in the left column with those in the right and to state the nature of the differences, if any.

I explicitly label both the process and the product of their thinking so that I can get them to produce thinking like this in the future.

The students inevitably produce lists with words like "formal," "dignified," "stately," and "calm" to describe Kennedy's funeral and "barbaric," "wild," "disorderly" and "chaotic" to describe the Ayatollah's. Easily, they notice the connotative differences between the first set of words (positive) and the second (negative). I then ask them to imagine why anyone would behave the way the mourners at the Ayatollah's funeral are behaving (tearing at their clothes, clamoring to touch the shrouded body, weeping frantically). Most of them discover that they can understand these behaviors as the outward expressions of intense grief, which removes them from the category of "crazy" to the category of "interpretable" action.

When the students have relativized their point of view this far, I ask them to consider what Kennedy's funeral would look like to one of the mourners at the Ayatollah's funeral. They get the point right away that Americans look "cold," "mechanical," and "unfeeling" to people whose cultural expectations differ from our own.

Finally I tell the students that they have just gone through a dialogic process to arrive at a relativized understanding of mourning behavior. That is, I explicitly label both the process and the product of their thinking so that I can get them to produce thinking like this in the future. I also point out where they have generalized and abstracted to arrive at where they are, and then I get them to talk about the relationship between description, interpretation and political or cultural stances. This generally launches wonderful discussion of subjectivity and objectivity, which are crucial concepts in contemporary thinking.

Bonnie Kendall
Anthropology
IU Bloomington

Questioning Authority

Having been born and raised in a very traditional Catholic family where my father was viewed by many, including myself, as a pillar of the church, it came as a profound and enormously empowering experience in college to be exposed to a Jesuit priest who modeled that it was OK to question even the most fundamental aspects of my belief system.

I recall with a clarity as if it were yesterday, his opening remark in a required religion course. He asked, "If there is a God, why do or should we assume she is benevolent?" This was my first substantial introduction to critical thinking. *For the first time in my formal education I realized that it was OK to question even the most basic of my prior beliefs. The willingness of this important role model to share his own uncertainty was very empowering in the sense that I felt I had been given permission to express my doubts and uncertainties. It was OK to risk.*

I recall that magic moment vividly and strive to convey that same sense of healthy skepticism to my own students.

Jerry Powers
Social Work
IUPUI

Leadership Style

When I began my teaching career, I erroneously believed that it was necessary to increase my "psychological size" to be an effective, credible teacher. I have discovered that my students are actually inhibited by their perception of me as a powerful figure and that my teaching is enhanced if I avoid the "chairman's" seat in a conference room, admit my limitations, and increase my learners' psychological size (i.e. encouraging them to be the teachers whenever possible, involving them in prioritizing and/or selecting relevant content to be learned).

Learning to Articulate Beliefs

Education students are given ample opportunity to discuss and write about their emerging philosophies. This is a good and necessary step in their development. They must also have experience in learning to clearly articulate their philosophies. This is necessary preparation for both job interviews and successful interaction with the many constituencies to whom teachers are responsible.

In two contexts, I develop interview questions and conduct interviews with students. One interview is based on social studies issues (E325) and the other is based on standard interview questions (M314). In both instances we take class time to explore various answers to the questions and to discuss interview strategies.

● I role play the principal's possible responses to questions and potential probing questions.

● The interviews are formally conducted with individual students in my office. Each interview lasts approximately 20 minutes.

● We share observations immediately following the interview. For the first few semesters, the student and I would determine his/her points together. For the past two semesters, the interviews have not been graded. Rather, students don't receive a grade for the semester until they have completed the interview. This places emphasis on the experience.

Student response to the interviews has been very positive. I originally devised this plan as one means of creating options for student assessment. Within two semesters, all students were opting for this experience. While admittedly nervous, it provides them with an opportunity to practice articulating beliefs in a relatively safe and supportive environment. Although the interviews take a great deal of time, it appears to be time well spent.

Marilyn Watkins
Education
IU East

Creating Enthusiasm

Students' evaluation of my teaching style over the past twenty years has typically indicated that I am empathetic, knowledgeable, and organized. They indicate that I give well illustrated lectures; but they also show that students desire more time for questions and discussion. I used to think they knew too little to have a meaningful discussion over the facts, theories, and principles of science, so I reorganized my classes, honed my presentation, clarified my lectures and <u>nothing</u> seemed to help.

Two activities, suggested by Craig Nelson (Biology, IU Bloomington, Critical Thinking workshop leader), have made an enormous difference in student participation, their enthusiasm for earth science, their awareness of its impact on their lives, and their desire to understand at a deeper level.

❧Ask each student to write a short explanation or answer to a question (one minute) followed by a one-on-one discussion and explanation between pairs of students. They do not report their discussion to the class but do have to express an answer and hear a different answer from another student.

❧Put a multiple choice question from an old exam on the board or screen; divide the class into groups of four or five; and have them discuss the adequacy and deficiency of each possible answer to the question. Then have one student from each group report on their discussion about understanding the topic being questioned. This student discussion takes about five minutes. You can keep the reporting short or let it run if the discussion is useful.

Bob Votaw
Geology
IU Northwest

History Is Real

In teaching the history of the Vietnam War (H228) to a broad spectrum of students, I have devised an assignment that achieves a variety of objectives.

➤Each student is required to locate one of the three thousand Vietnam War veterans in Allen county, interview the veteran, and write a paper based on the interview.

➤I provide background information on interviewing and a consent form that must be signed by the veteran. This form permits the veteran to select the level of confidentiality he or she prefers and legitimizes the request for the interview.

While apprehensive at first, I have been amazed that virtually no one solicited for an interview has turned a student down or has become disenchanted along the way.

From this assignment students derive various benefits:

➤The realization that "History" is real and involves real people at a local level as well as in distant places.

➤The exercise of listening, thinking, and writing skills.

➤The development of judgment skills in comparing specific life experiences against the generalizations of various history texts.

➤Improved understanding of the vast variety of war experiences compared to the narrow range generally emphasized in war literature.

➤Understanding of the significant difference between real life experiences and film portrayals of the war.

➤Realization that a war is not over when the last shot is fired.

By the time we discuss the experiences of Vietnam troops and veterans, students have a wide background of information to share. Interest is quite keen.

Veterans who are interviewed appear to have benefitted significantly from the assignment as well. Many remark that this is the first time anyone has shown interest in their experience or that they have spoken seriously
about the war to anyone outside their immediate family.

In several cases, students have maintained a warm personal relationship with the
person interviewed.

In addition, the Vet Center and the local chapter of the Vietnam Veterans of American support the interviews (and by extension, the university). In a small way the interviews help veterans come out of the many closets quite a number have lived in.

There are other benefits from the assignment:

➤On the consent form, veterans are asked if they are willing to have their interviews placed in a special Vietnam War file of the local county historical society. At least three-fourths of the veterans agree to this, although some place time conditions on the public use of their interviews.

➤I have built up in the local history archives a considerable source for future student war investigators who will not have available what my generation of students have had.

➤Two of my student interview papers have been printed in the county historical society quarterly, so they have already shed some light for the larger society.

A modest assignment can have a broad ripple of positive consequences.

Clifford Scott
History
Ft. Wayne

Say It Graphically

Every classroom teacher, kindergarten through college, consistently faces one basic challenge: every class is composed of students with varied learning styles. While lecture appeals to 10-20% of students who are auditory learners, the use of graphic organizers captures the attention of students across the learning styles spectrum: visual, auditory and kinesthetic. By clustering, detailing, and illustrating course content graphically and discussing the final product, teachers allow students to manipulate the information, see it visually displayed, and discuss or interpret the relationship between facts presented.

Every classroom teacher, kindergarten through college, consistently faces one basic challenge: every class is composed of students with varied learning styles.

Students enrolled in Reading Methods for Secondary Math, Science and Social Studies especially benefit from instruction in the use of graphic organizers because it is a strategy that crosses disciplines. These students undergo a three phase introduction to the process: exploration, discovery, and application. In the "exploration phase" students bring to class a secondary school text for their respective discipline. Once we have discussed the need for reading graphic symbols as well as reading word symbols, we explore the content area texts. Students are usually surprised by publishers' use of tables, graphs, matrixes, time lines, flow charts, and story maps. In fact, current publications are increasing the use of graphics to capture student interest. The exploration phase usually raises the awareness of preservice teachers and heightens their interest in discovering how they might incorporate the technique into their methodology.

In the "discovery phase" we look at and discuss six to eight graphic forms that are generic and are easily used in illustrating an understanding of a given topic. One such form is the "spider map." It is readily used when discussing a specific topic, theme, or concept. The topic is written in the center of the page, and ideas related to the topic branch of it. Detailing branches can be drawn from each idea statement. This provides a pictorial summary of facts related to the topic. A "series of events chain" plots the sequence or stages of a given

event story, or cycle. The step-by-step procedure allows students to capture the initiating event, subsequent actions, and the final outcome. This not only plots a sequence but allows for interpretation, analysis, and evaluation of the steps in the cycle that are significant to the outcome of the event. Another form which lends itself to versatility and solicits higher order reasoning is the "problem-solution outline." This frame requires students to define the problem, consider various solutions, and judge which solution results in the most satisfactory outcome.

Once students have explored and discovered the possible uses of graphic organizers, the "application phase" begins. Students are assigned articles on reading comprehension and/or vocabulary. The task is for each student to read an article and summarize its main idea using the most appropriate graphic organizer to illustrate the topic. Students are given a transparency and markers. They design the visual illustration of the assigned topic and present their graphic and oral interpretation to the class using an overhead projector.

I now have a collection of article summaries graphically represented which serve as excellent examples of the assignment for incoming groups of preservice teachers. The current class of preservice teachers have had the opportunity to see, hear, and do a technique with practical applications for all content areas and appeal for all learning styles.

Spider Map

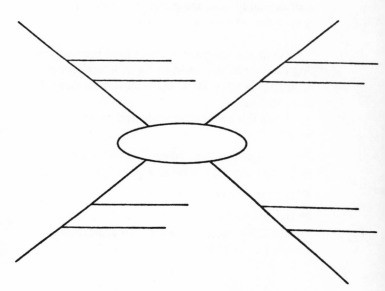

Series of Events Chain

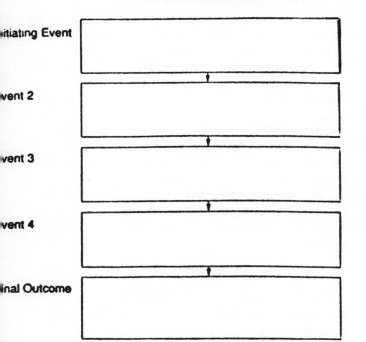

Initiating Event

Event 2

Event 3

Event 4

Final Outcome

Problem-Solution Frame

Problem

What is the problem?

Why is it a problem?

Who has the problem?

Solutions		Results

Solution

End Result

Kevin Sue Bailey
Education
IU Southeast

The Dangers of Typecasting

In my Vietnam War course I use two Vietnam vet friends to play against type casting. One vet is a large, athletic African American who was a Marine D.I., Gunny Sergeant, and platoon leader at Khe Sanh and elsewhere, who is gentle as a lamb, still with his first wife, no alcohol, no problems of adjustment; the other vet is a wisp of an Anglo, looks angelic, who went through seven kinds of hell after Vietnam, but who finally has everything pretty well together. Students see the widely varied impact of Vietnam on veterans, the dangers of type casting, and the general silliness of the mass media trash to which they are exposed.

Cliff Scott
History
IU Ft. Wayne

In my Vietnam War course...students see the widely varied impact of Vietnam on veterans, the dangers of type casting, and the general silliness of the mass media trash to which they are exposed.

Using Case Studies

Lots of us use case studies in our teaching. Students love them and respond more enthusiastically to concrete problems than to theoretical issues. However, as a teacher of ethics I have recently realized that cases are used in several different ways. In my experience, using cases has improved now that I understand exactly how I use them.

Cases are often used to illustrate some theoretical principle. The case functions as a tool to teach a broader theory. That's a legitimate use for cases, though one not always open to new ways of interpreting the case. Some instructors using cases for this purpose "know" where the discussion should lead and tend to reject student analyses of cases which head in other directions. At its worst, this leads to a phony Socratic dialogue, denigrating student insight and learning.

Cases can also be used for exactly the opposite purpose: to demonstrate the futility of theory and principles for resolving concrete problems. In the context of values, this is situation ethics; in other fields, it is intellectual relativism.

I have found a third way to use cases more satisfying than the first two options. Casuistry, or case-based reasoning, begins with cases, not theory. This inductive "bottom-up" approach takes cases seriously as a place where we can all learn about the problems of our fields. Unlike the first approach, one cannot be sure where the case analysis will lead. One needs to be open to new interpretations -- to changing your theoretical perspective rather than proving it. In other words, the case helps us develop new insights into theory and principles.

One can build this perspective into major assignments for courses. In place of a term paper in my senior-level ethics class, students carry out a case-based reasoning process in three steps: the development of a rich case description; crafting guidelines for this case and similar cases; and identifying theoretical principles found in the guidelines.

For example, analysis of the William Kennedy Smith /Patricia Bowman case can lead to a general guideline on naming rape victims in future cases. Comparing that case with other rape trials refines the operating guideline. Finally, the guidelines themselves reflect basic values: privacy, fairness, the public good.

We still get to the theory, but in a way that is more interesting and more open to taking student's views -- and cases -- seriously.

Dave Boeyink
Journalism
IU Bloomington

The Hermeneutical Approach

In teaching foreign concepts, I attempt to be hermeneutical, creating understanding by drawing connections between my students' world and the world I would have them understand. For example, in teaching about the origins of rhetorical theory in the ancient world, I adapt to my students' situations. Some background on this topic is necessary: rhetorical theory was first developed by Corax of Syracuse in the early 5th Century BC after the fall of a dictatorship that destroyed property records. In the absence of deeds, claimants in courts (who had to represent themselves) had to rely upon arguments from probability to establish their ownership. Corax adapted to this need by teaching and writing a book on probable argument.

To explain this development and give students an understanding of how rhetorical theory grew out of practical needs, I begin this lesson with a hypothetical situation: an earthquake has destroyed the Howard County Courthouse and all property records were lost. Someone makes a claim against your property and, since many lawyers lost their lives in the disaster (a point that brings a laugh), you must defend your property rights in court. What will you do? What will you say?

After they "discover" arguments from probability on their own, I ask whether any enterprising students see a business opportunity here (i.e., to teach others how to argue this way). Allowing students to figure out how one might argue and adapt to the need to argue rather than merely reporting the historical fact makes the learning more memorable, enjoyable, and understandable.

I begin with a hypothetical situation: an earthquake has destroyed the Howard County Courthouse and all property records were lost.

This approach is hermeneutical in adapting to the recent media attention given to the New Madrid fault which threatens Indiana and in helping students understand "from the inside" why rhetorical theory would develop. When I taught at the University of Georgia I used the example of Sherman's destruction "twenty miles wide to the Gulf of Mexico" to create the circumstance of destroyed deeds, offering a cultural setting with which they could identify.

This approach is obviously adaptable to teaching any historically or culturally distant concepts. A variation would use the analogical process it involves to explain difficult concepts. For example, I sometimes use the commonplace example for "choices you have to make in preparing for a dinner party" to introduce the notion of rhetorical choices involving invention, arrangement, style, and delivery (whereby "adapting to guests" becomes "adapting to audience," "culinary style" becomes "rhetorical style," "table arrangement" and "dinner courses" become "the arrangement of speech parts," etc.

J. Clarke Rountree, III
Rhetorical Studies /Communication
IU Kokomo

Mind Mapping

By surveying students during the first class meeting of R200, Nursing Research each semester, I have found that they prejudge this course as being overly difficult and utterly boring. Although I do not expect students to have the same passion for research that I do, I make it my teaching mission to create a learning atmosphere that promotes critical thinking, curiosity, and a beginning understanding of and respect for the research process.

This past Fall Semester I introduced **mind mapping** which seemed to be an extremely effective method. After I presented a unit of content in the traditional lecture format, students participated in **mind mapping** activities which verified that they understood the content presented.

This technique involves one student at the blackboard who, aided by classmates, draws the content in model format. (See **mind mapping** samples on the next page). While classmates help the individual at the blackboard depict the content in model form, I have the opportunity to clarify any misconceptions or misunderstandings. This also provides a unique learning opportunity for visual learners as well as those who learn and retain best when they talk through content. Students are also actively involved with their own learning process.

The class quickly becomes acclimated to this type of synthesis activity and eagerly volunteers to be the recorder. The models become more creative as the semester progresses and students seem to enjoy participating.

I found the introduction of this teaching strategy particularly rewarding when one student stopped me during the middle of presenting a difficult concept and said, "Could we stop here a minute and mind map this?" This was one of those special moments in teaching when one feels as if everything has clicked and the students are assuming responsibility for their own learning!!!

Linda Rooda
Nursing
Northwest

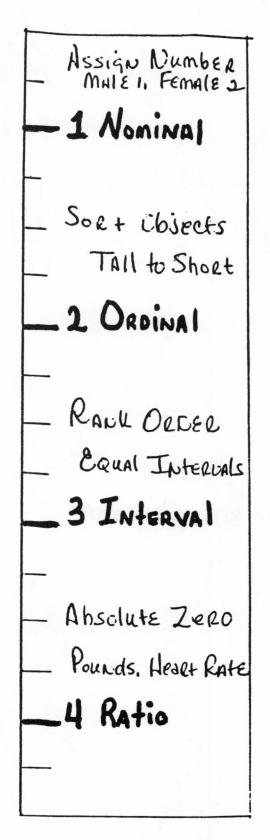

LEVELS OF MEASUREMENT

Assign Number
Male 1, Female 2
1 Nominal

Sort objects
Tall to Short
2 Ordinal

Rank Order
Equal Intervals
3 Interval

Absolute Zero
Pounds, Heart Rate
4 Ratio

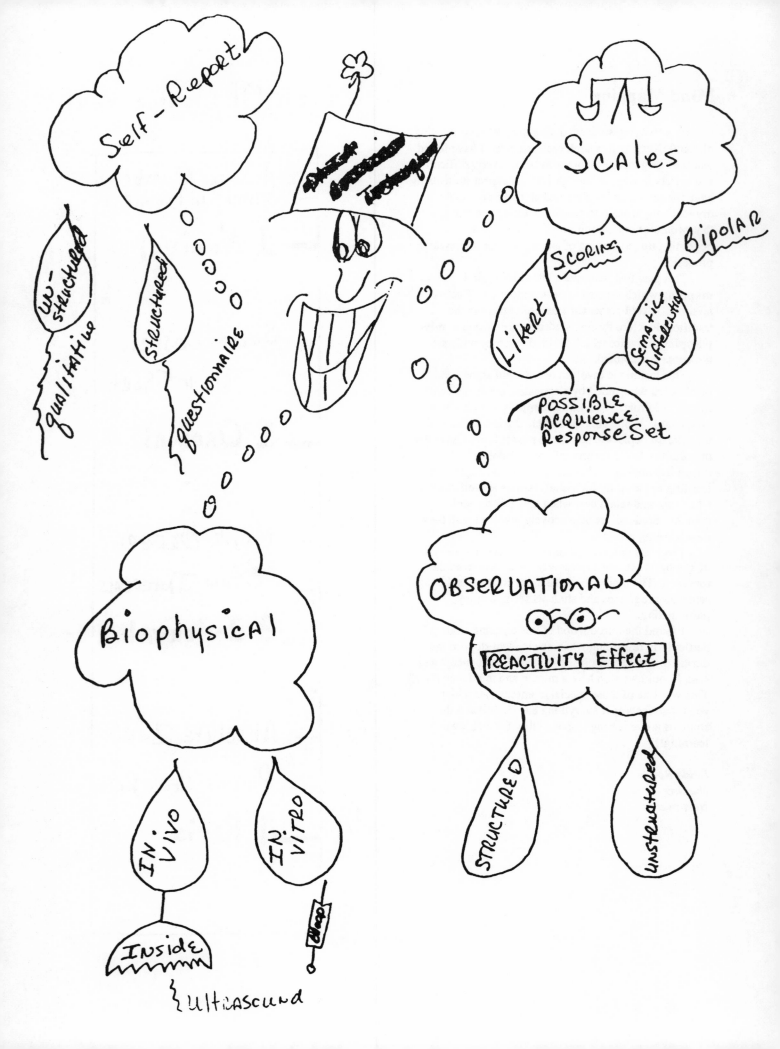

Motivating Students to Think Critically

To teach critical thinking, which is what I would like to think I'm about in all my classes, I try to encourage the students to engage another thinker directly, without mediation.

In teaching the Letters of Paul, I am helped by the fact that Paul himself is such an interesting and provocative thinker.

To teach critical thinking, which is what I would like to think I'm about in all my classes, I try to encourage the students to engage another thinker directly, without mediation.

Students are required to write three papers in sequence: the first is a straight research project, reporting on how some aspect of Paul's symbolic world influenced his thinking (Stoicism, Pharisaism, etc.); the second is a direct interpretation of a passage in one of Paul's Letters, chosen by me to yield only to careful analysis. Students are not allowed to use the interpretations of others, but must employ the basic methods of textual analysis: determining context, structure, argument, etc. Then, the final paper is a critical response to another reader's interpretation (one of the "greats" in the field). That interpretation is subjected to the same criteria I have applied to their own research.

This progression in assignments seems to give students confidence in their ability to think for themselves, especially when they realize that I consistently reward the ability to make an argument for a position rather than maintaining a "correct" position.

Luke Johnson
Religious Studies
IU Bloomington

Modifying Instructor Behavior to Student Needs

When I focus on my own conscious strategies in the classroom, three elements come to mind:

1. I constantly refine my techniques and learn from past experiences, and I never teach a class exactly the same way in subsequent semesters. Before writing up a new syllabus, I review student evaluations from past semesters, study the notes I wrote to myself regarding tasks or approaches that succeeded or failed, and consciously add exercises, a new text, etc.

2. I experiment with my teaching. When I was asked to teach our graduate-level Bibliography and Methods of Research course (potentially a real bore) last semester, I decided to base the class on what I would most have liked to know about the profession when I was a graduate student. I structured the course around three units: how to use our research facilities and current technologies to do research; how to write and document scholarly papers in our field; and what it means to be a member of the profession (ethics, how to prepare a c.v., the job market, etc.) The experiment worked.

3. I go with the flow. I always encourage a lot of class discussion, but I like to be flexible enough to deviate from my plans when doing so is profitable for the students. In a recent undergraduate course on staging Spanish Golden Age drama, three students decided to get creative with their short papers. They wrote such clever parodies of Don Juan plays (in verse - and in Spanish!) that we decided as a group to perform them for the department. The students learned a lot about the theater in the process, and although we short-changed two texts that I had included on the syllabus, their original productions were a great trade-off. Although I feel most comfortable working within a structured environment, I know that if I had shackled those students to the syllabus, we would all have missed out on a wonderful experience.

Catherine Larson
Spanish and Portuguese
IU Bloomington

Reacting to Student Boredom

Eyes on the clock; daydreaming; stifled yawns; restlessness. We've all experienced these student reactions from time to time. The students are bored with the lecture and perhaps the course itself has lost its challenge. Or alternatively, we are teaching far above our students' level of comprehension. To me, this is one of teaching's most unnerving experiences: knowing you are not communicating!

Reacting to student body language is important in demonstrating a sincere desire to give students the opportunity to get maximum benefit from the course.

Although I have been fortunate not to have faced this situation often, when it has occurred, I have been flexible enough to change tactics on the fly. In two separate instances, I made substantial course revisions and changed the thrust of the course content to satisfy the technical demands of my students. In another case, I found it necessary to devote two weeks to laying a scientific foundation that most students lacked.

Reacting to student body language is important in demonstrating a sincere desire to give students the opportunity to get maximum benefit from the course.

Robert Orr
Computer Technology
IUPUI

Countering Student Resistance to Course Topic

T351 is the fifth and final course in a required sequence of music theory/literature courses in which students develop an understanding of Western art music, focusing on the 1700-1900 "common practice" period. This final semester, however, deals exclusively with 20th-century music. It still amazes me how conservative many undergraduate music majors are. A large percentage have already come to the conclusion that there is nothing of value for them to hear or learn in the last 90 years! Unfortunately, a number of their private performance instructors reinforce the notion - explicitly or implicitly - in the music they perform on their own recitals, that "good" music died about 1900.

T351 is the first core music course in which students work with a faculty member in groups of 30 or less, and by this time they have grown accustomed to being silently anonymous in large lecture sections. They start the semester ill-at-ease in such close contact with a professor. Dutifully they put up with the music they hear, memorizing facts about composers and pieces, keeping their opinions to themselves. But, at some point in the semester - you never know when - somebody who has been silent thus far cannot contain him/herself anymore. "Why are we wasting our time on this junk? This isn't music!"

It still amazes me how conservative many undergraduate music majors are. A large percentage have already come to the conclusion that there is nothing of value to hear or learn in the last 90 years!

Forget about anything you had planned to do during this hour. Put aside lecture notes. With as little interference as possible, stimulate conversation among class members. Students begin to question one another - themselves - as to what music is. "It can't be music if there are only percussion instruments" was the spark which ignited one class. Ultimately, everyone is forced to articulate and re-evaluate long-held opinions about music, about the respective roles of composer and performer, and about aesthetics. This represents a turning point in the semester from passive learning to active involvement. The instructor needs to watch for this moment and be flexible enough to nourish it.

Gary Potter
Music theory
IU Bloomington

Audience

The cardinal rule for excellent writing is to think first about the intended audience. A crucial component of excellent teaching involves a similar proposition: think about the composition of the class, about what the students already know, about what they do not know, and about what they do not need to know.

Among the worst mistakes I used to make in teaching introductory courses was to pitch the course to the audience that I imagined was there rather than to the people actually out there in front of me. The introductory course I currently teach does not count toward a major in my department. Consequently, I have to assume - and constantly have to remind the Associate Instructors to assume - that the students enrolled in the course may have no particular interest in, and may have no reason to have an interest in, the details and complexities of my field.

Among the worst mistakes I used to make in teaching introductory courses was to pitch the course to the audience that I imagined was there rather than to the people actually out there in front of me.

(If I could assume that the students in the course were going to major in my discipline, I would have to structure the course accordingly.) This seems to me so obvious that it should go unsaid, but, in fact, it is easy to lose sight of. Too many people construct their introductory courses as if the audience were composed of people highly committed to their discipline. The results are frequently dreadful.

I build on students' interest to engage their interest. Head-phones and Walkmen are now standard dress on campuses throughout the United States. And because music is so much a part of the lives of contemporary college students, it is a natural device for promoting interaction and community among class members. I play exotic music (Tibetan Buddhist chants, Hopi Indiana rain prayers, Indiana ragas, Afro-Brazilian trance songs, Ghanian highlife tunes) over the auditorium's sound system before and after my classes. I stroll around the room and answer students' questions about the music. This works quite naturally in an anthropology class, but there is no

principled reason why is shouldn't work for any other variety of large class. The point of importing music into the classroom is to share an experience, to create a bond. A surprising number of students tell me that they come to class early out of sheer curiosity about the music of the day.

Occasionally, I use the first five minutes of a class to project a thematic slide show set to popular music (e.g., Cocker's You Are So Beautiful as the musical accompaniment to a series of slides on body adornment, preceding a participatory lecture on beauty; Mellancamp's Authority as the background to a set of slides depicting institutions of prelude to a class on social order). Occasionally, I use musical slide shows during the last five minutes of the class as a way of summarizing the day's points. Sometimes during exams I play Sati or Debussy.

Bonnie Kendall
Anthropology
IU Bloomington

Group Activities to Promote Teamwork

Group activities and projects seem to keep students more involved and, in nighttime courses, more alert as well. Such activities have included take-home examinations in which only some answers are in assigned texts; group analysis of situational case studies; design and programming projects that are both extensive and of professional caliber (that is, the problems are of practical rather than academic value); and role playing exercises.

At the same time, I have created grading standards that include both individual and group grades. This action tends to keep all students "honest" in their efforts to make worthwhile contributions.

Robert Orr
Computer Technology
IUPUI

Skipping the Survey Text

In introductory courses, skip the survey text if possible. In the last decade and a half, the introductory texts in many fields have shown a marked diminution in interest and a marked increase in similarity. Bland and homogeneous, they skirt controversy by representing a discipline's concepts and definitions as bodies of uncontested "givens" rather than as focus of lively dialogue. In short, they stifle controversy, thereby discouraging critical reasoning.

My goal is to get students to think of anthropology as a critical stance, an approach to problems, a way of reasoning, rather than as a body of knowledge.

In the Intro course I've been developing over the past twelve years, I assign four or five paperback books, none of which is explicitly written as a text--and only one or two of which are written by members of my discipline. I select them on the basis of readability and framing problematic, and I talk students through them with the aim of illustrating how people in my field think about problems which the books broach. Last semester, for example, I assigned a paperback on the aftermath of experiments where humans attempted to teach sign language to chimpanzees. We used the book as the point of departure for discussing how humans think about animals, how they conceive their relationship to other forms of life and what consequences follow from those conceptions. A book on obsessive eating disorders served as the backdrop for discussing the politics and economics of beauty, the interconnectedness of self and society, the symbolism of control in American life. Neither book was written by an anthropologist, yet both covered issues with which my discipline concerns itself. This allowed me to make explicit contrast between how the author approached the subject at hand and how I, as an anthropologist, have been trained to think about it.

My goal is to get students to think of anthropology as a critical stance, an approach to problems, a way of reasoning, rather than as a body of knowledge. Survey textbooks often present the products of disciplinary thinking, rather than its processes. Thus they fail to illuminate the distinguishing feature of disciplinary modes of thought.

Bonnie Kendall
Anthropology
IU Bloomington

Product/Process

Generating class discussion can sometimes be a challenge. I've developed a presentation on "Education as product (emphasis on 'credentials') and process (emphasis on personal growth and development)" that usually works as a catalyst for discussion. Specifically, I ask the class to apply the "product/process" distinction to their own experiences in school. I also ask them to consider what they have learned in school in addition to formal subjects. This usually gets students to talk about gender roles, race relations, power/authority/ bureaucracy, and family and peer-group conflicts. I try with each topic to tap into the students" own experiences and interpretations. Sometimes, if students don't feel like talking, I'll offer my own experience as a discussion starter. This strategy is usually successful.

Rich Aniskiewicz
Computer Technology
IU Kokomo

Instead of Midterm or Final Exams...

In a class based on structured discussion, student remarks can focus on personal experience and observation rather than the assigned reading. This is particularly a problem in courses like the family or women and work.

If the class is a long one (e.g., a "one-shot" class which meets two hours and 40 minutes), I assign a paper or give a quiz during each class on the assigned reading. I then do not give midterm or final exams. This, of course, means the students have to have done the reading.

This means a substantial amount of grading for me, but it is generally worth it. Students' personal experience and observations can easily be analyzed in light of the reading. Attendance also improves.

Linda Haas
Sociology/Women's Studies
IUPUI

Collaborative Exams

Give exams that require critical thinking. Most intro textbooks come with Instructor's Guides providing selections of multiple choice, true/false and essay exam questions. They make exam construction easy. However, the so-called "objective" questions in these Instructor's Guides generally require only the lowest level of mental skill from students, while the essay questions rarely demand anything more complicated than comparison. Pre-fab exams do little to foster the students' intellectual development, because they neither teach nor challenge, which is a major argument against them.

With a class enrollment of three hundred students, machine-scored exams are almost unavoidable, so the problem is to write thought-provoking objective questions that exercise the students' critical capacities.

On the other hand, with a class enrollment of three hundred students, machine-scored exams are almost unavoidable, so the problem is to write thought-provoking objective questions that exercise the students' critical capacities. I've evolved the following system, which works very well.

The first exam is a multiple-choice collaborative take-home. The students have one week to work out the answers. I tell them that they are required to refer to their books and to consult each other; I generally suggest that they work in groups.

The questions are deliberately challenging, requiring close scrutiny of assigned readings and mastery of materials presented in class. Some items refer to specific text passages and ask for the most plausible interpretation; some demand that connections be made between readings and lectures; some require the students to compare one author's implicit assumptions to another's; most require evaluation of evidence in support of assertions.

After having had a week to puzzle over and discuss the exams, in class the students fill out scantrons or bubble-sheets with their responses. On exam day, they are also required to write out justifications for five of their answers on separate pieces of paper and turn these in with the scantrons. They do not know in advance which answers they will be asked to justify, although

they are made to understand that the justifications will be scored and will count as 20% of their total grade on the test. The point of this exercise is to encourage students to take the exam seriously, i.e., (1) to make them think deeply about why they answered the way they did and (2) to discourage them from "cheating," which in this context means relying on others to do their thinking for them.

The second exam, like the first, is a machine-scored collaborative exercise emphasizing critical thinking. The third exam is also machine-scored, collaborative exercise emphasizing critical thinking. It is also machine-scored, but is taken individually in class with no separate answer justifications. The final exercise is an essay exam.

The first two exams teach the students the high level of reasoning that is expected from them. The third exam asks them to manifest it on their own. The final essay questions, which are printed in the syllabus, require the students to integrate and apply what they have learned in various ways.

Students inevitably comment on their course evaluations that the exams are challenging but fair, and that they learn much about critical reading and critical thinking in debating the answers to the first two exams with their classmates.

Bonnie Kendall
Anthropology
IU Bloomington

Thinking Mathematically

Elementary math students learn the theory of math education, but sometimes have difficulty applying it.

In an effort to extend theory into practice and encourage reflective observation and critical thinking, I ask my elementary math methods students to select an elementary-aged student at the beginning of the semester. Throughout the semester, they observe and talk with this student to discover how children think mathematically.

Students observe and talk with an elementary student to discover how children think mathematically.

They keep a journal that records what they have learned about their child's thinking, how they planned to solve one learning problem the student had, and the methods they used to accomplish the task. In the latter part of the semester, we share this information with each other, also sharing possible alternative methods and solutions. This experience allows university students to integrate experiential discovery of practice while learning the theory that undergirds appropriate practice. This is a more powerful learning experience than either exposure separately.

Carol S. Browne
Elementary Education
IU East

Strategies for Teaching Western Civilization and History

Indiana secondary schools do not require world or European history. In Western Civilization I must present 4500 years of history encompassing 35 plus countries to students who have America-centric viewpoints and not the foggiest notion of geography.

✈ I use many visuals from my travels to illustrate the heritage of the region's studies. This gives immediacy and stimulates questions.

✈ I require passing a map quiz , but permit students to take it as often as necessary. This structures studying, reduces grade anxiety by using P/F grading.

✈ I use role-playing problem-solving essays to develop analytical writing skills. This emphasizes cause-and-effect relationships instead of simple date replication.

Eleanor Turk
History
IU East

Collaboration in Research Methods

I teach a social science research methods class. The material is completely new to students and, while they eventually understand the main concepts, in the past they were unable to apply their new knowledge to actual research situations. The final paper requires them to develop an original research proposal, and the quality of the papers was low.

I established collaborative learning groups to complete exercises designed to apply the reading to new situations.

I established collaborative learning groups to complete exercises designed to apply the reading to new situations.

I circulated around the room and gave as much help on the exercise as they wanted. Groups turned in written reports for a grade, and individual contributions to group work were evaluated by peers at the end of the semester.

Students enjoyed learning from peers very much. Although it was not my intention, course evaluations were much more positive. The quality of the final papers improved dramatically.

Linda Haas
Sociology/Women's Studies
IUPUI

Medicine: Diagnosing Endocrine Disorders Via Patient Interviews

Teaching medical students to diagnose endocrine disorders is difficult because they must identify and analyze a number of non-specific symptoms and physical exam abnormalities. One or two isolated findings are not adequate to establish a diagnosis; it's the group or clustering of signs and symptoms that is important. For the beginning student, this means memorizing lists of diagnostic clues, and retaining this knowledge often can be difficult.

Patient interviews allow reinforcement of the signs and symptoms that must be identified and analyzed.

We have found it useful to prepare an Endocrine corebook (professor's notes) that explains why various signs and symptoms occur. We then use classroom time to interview patients with various endocrine disorders. Students read the factual information found in the corebook prior to lecture. Patient interviews then allow reinforcement of the signs and symptoms that must be identified and analyzed. This also allows students in the classroom to actively participate and practice their problem-solving skills.

Richard Powell
Medicine
IUPUI

Teaching "The World in the 20th Century" in One Semester to Prospective Teachers.

✳Focus on regions rather than countries; analytical terms rather than chronology.

✳Extend content coverage by assigning students collaborative reports rather than individual term papers.

✳Incorporate PC Globe Software to produce individual and regional maps, demographic and economic databases on demand as student investigation progresses.

✳Require student journals that discuss current news on their region.

✳Collecting articles which do not analyze from the American perspective.

✳Emphasize collaboration by requiring each student to critique all other oral presentations, based on a critique form handed out in advance. (This also sensitizes perspective teachers to variations in student performance.)

Eleanor Turk
History
IU East

Philosophy of Teaching and Learning

Direct Communication

One challenge I had early in my career involved a perception by my students that I wasn't particularly enthusiastic about my teaching. They indicated on their evaluations that I seemed to be only moderately interested in my subject (usually literature). That disturbed me because I knew it wasn't true. I loved reading and discussing literature, and I wanted them to share my feeling. So I decided to convey my love more overtly, to "exclaim" over passages in our reading that were especially powerful or brilliant more openly about the admiration I felt for these writers.

Students indicated on their evaluations that I seemed to be only moderately interested in my subject (usually literature). That disturbed me because I knew it wasn't true.

Surprisingly to me, this seemed to work. The evaluations now spoke much about my enthusiasm. So I think I learned something valuable from this experience; you often need to be very direct and explicit to communicate successfully with your students, and simple, obvious solutions are sometimes the best.

Another challenge I might mention is the uncertainty and even hostility that students often bring to a freshman literature class. Many of them had avoided reading serious literature in high school and seemed to feel that it had no interest for them or that they had no idea what it was about. My solution was to reduce somewhat the amount of reading, but more importantly to encourage them in various ways that they could understand it and that it did have relevance to their lives.

I would proceed slowly step-by-step from the text to the ideas, and then raise questions about what is meant for our lives. Here the older students often had remarkable insights to offer because of their greater experience. Of course, this is a continual reassurance that they can grasp what is going on in the stories and poems, and seems to work with most students.

Nick Nelson
English
Kokomo

Leadership and the Classroom Environment

Each class presents a different scenario. Professors must be leaders. The class is like any other organization. It has a mission, a set of resources, and a methodology. The students are your charges - yours to mold, motivate, and educate. If a student fails to learn, then you both have done something wrong.

By applying the principles of leadership, you create a climate that is conductive to learning. It is your task to motivate your students to want to learn. Since students respond to different leadership techniques, you must ascertain the best way to reach each student. Some will be self-motivators who require only inspiration, others need to be lead - to be shown the way to success; still others need to be pushed, encouraged, and even chastised privately.

By setting an example for your students, you become a role model. I have found that organizations quickly adopt the personality of their leaders. This is true to a great extent in the classroom. If you are professional in your approach, prepared, organized, thorough, understanding and concerned about the progress of your students, they likewise will put forth the effort necessary to complete the course successfully. As long as students see the purpose in what they are being asked to do, they will respond. Therefore, make it clear from day one exactly what you expect from each student.

Robert Orr
Computer Technology
IUPUI

Overcoming Students' Limitations

Overcoming students' limitations and putting their energy and enthusiasm to good use are big challenges. Briefly, I have tried to handle these challenges by asking and answering the following questions:

1. Why do students take my class?

Perhaps to fulfill a degree requirement - or because they like my subject. I have realized that it is not for the love of the class alone.

2. What is the student's capacity?

They are all different, have different work habits, memory, background, etc. I can't do anything about their memory and intelligence. I begin with the assumption that my students are the best my university can attract.

3. Do my students need encouragement?

They may lack confidence. I usually encourage them by guiding them through the curriculum. Since students are all different, I deal with them individually, but they like to see the teacher's feedback, and need attention.

4. How can I develop each student's ability?

I try to give them suitable assignments, responsibility, and make them think and work diligently. Every student has ability that could be developed. But it needs patience.

5. How does the student learn in my class?

I stress fundamentals and teach the facts as a foundation; then I try to apply them to real world problems. Also, I try to show different examples until students see the whole picture.

6. How quickly do students absorb new knowledge?

Students are different in absorption. Some are slow, some are quick. But all students need time to relate a new concept to what they already know.

Morteza Shafii-Mousavi
Mathematics
IU South Bend

Resistance to Remedial Courses

T506 is graduate remedial sightsinging course for those with poor undergraduate preparation in singing music at sight, a skill useful for all musicians. After failing the exemption test, many (most) students enter the course resentfully.

I try to put myself in the student's place. Instead of fighting their resentment, I tell them that I understand it. At the first class meeting, I list the "Top 10 Reasons You Probably Wish You Weren't Here." The list changes from time to time, but it might include:

1. I regard this course as an obstacle between me and my musical goals. It will set back my degree progress.

2. It's an expense I hadn't planned.

3. I don't think this is a skill I'll ever use after this course.

4. This stuff is boring.

5. Sightsinging has been traumatic for me in the past.

6. Either you can do it or you can't. It's not something you can learn in a course.

7. I could have passed this test but my skills were a bit rusty.

8. I could have passed the test, but I just freaked out. This was my first week in a completely new environment and I blew it.

9. It's embarrassing to go off to grad school and be thrown into remedial sightsinging.

10. I was the best student in my undergrad music department. It's an ego shock to come here to be just one of several hundred fine performers. My undergrad teachers praised my sightsinging because I was the best they had there in years. I believe that IU's expectations are unrealistically high.

Gary Potter
Music Theory
IU Bloomington

Teaching With International Perspective

American students of contemporary world history, politics and economics face three major problems in the information age. First, they lack a **comprehensive personal knowledge base** of geography and current events on which to build these studies. Most American newspapers present the international news in terms of articles digested from wire-service reports. The electronic media proudly proclaim, "give us twenty-two minutes and we'll give you the world." The popular news magazines simply amplify these techniques.

Despite the flood of articles and broadcasts, the United States public, and our students, are increasingly under-informed about world affairs in the information age.

Second, the stories in the major media often present strongly **America-centric viewpoints**. We are usually ignorant of the perspectives important to other countries because, as a nation, we lack the language skills to obtain them first hand. As a result, we fail to understand the underlying causes of their policies and problems, and often lack respect for the legitimacy of their actions. Finally, we lack the **statistical literacy** necessary to make meaningful analytical comparisons of data. Thus, despite the flood of

articles and broadcasts, the United States public, and our students, are increasingly **under-informed** about world affairs in the information age.

The challenge for the instructor is not only to contend with the data deficits through course content, but also to inculcate in the students an appreciation for the legitimacy of alternate, often conflicting foreign viewpoints, and then to equip them with ways of finding and analyzing those perspectives. This is a particular challenge to me in my course, "The World in the Twentieth Century," because it is intended to help education majors meet their "global studies" requirement. The information, methods and attitudes developed through their work in this course have the implications for the students whom they will teach.

The course requirements answer that challenge. The **text**, while conveying the usual chronologies, emphasizes five themes for analyzing world events. Students are required to keep a **print media journal** of current events based on two articles per week, but may discuss only articles which deal with foreign policy. All students must pass a **map quiz**, which emphasizes physical geography and world capitols listed on a map key which I provide as a study guide. The research component centers on a **collaborative group report** which presents one of four world regions (Latin America, Africa, the Middle East and Asia) from the perspective of one of the analytical

themes.

The media journal raises the first red flag. Students find that their usual newspapers and magazines seldom present significant information on other states from a neutral or foreign perspective. This sets them on the search for alternative media. They discover resources like the <u>Christian Science Monitor</u>, the <u>World Press Review</u>, and even the <u>Moscow News</u>. The value of this search is that it forces students to consider the reasons for other perspectives; it also provides a basis for comparative analysis. Often, in order to make that analysis, students must seek out informative data bases, such as almanacs, yearbooks and atlases. This makes them aware of the breadth of information needed to make an informed judgment. There is usually considerable class discussion about whether or not the print media is comprehensive enough to lead public opinion responsibly.

To emphasize learning over grades, I provide students with a study key. They may take the quiz as often as needed to pass it.

Students must pass a map quiz in order to pass the course. The quiz, consisting of 50 items, is administered in class at the beginning of the third week and graded Pass/Fail (P=80% or 40 items). This is a daunting assignment for most, since, in Indiana 60% of high school graduates have not had a course in geography or world history. To emphasize learning over grades, I provide students with a study key. They may take the quiz as often as needed to pass it, as long as they complete the requirement by the last scheduled day of class. To retake the quiz, students must schedule an appointment in my office hours. This provides me with an opportunity to review their study procedures and provide additional studying hints. After eight years of using this methodology in all my courses, to date only three students have failed the course because of the map quiz.

The text, media journal and map quiz help students acquire the necessary knowledge base for understanding current history. In class, I use another resource which offers them a substantial analytical tool. That is a computer program, PCGLOBE4.0, published by PC Globe, Inc., Tempe AZ. Available commercially, this program combines map graphics and statistical data bases for 190 countries and regions of the world. It produces maps, bar charts and tables of current statistics on individual countries, and compares up to eleven countries. I introduce it to the class through printed handouts and overhead projections to help them grasp problems such as inadequate economic resources or trade, the implications of rapid population growth, and the values reflected in national investment for education, health, and defense. Students soon realize that this software is also a valuable resource for their collaborative classroom reports.

The collaborative report helps acquaint these education majors with the various steps necessary to teach a class. In the second week

of class, the students are divided into the four regional research groups. Henceforth their media journals focus on that region. They meet weekly in class to review recent events, relate them to the curse themes, and plan their presentation. Utilizing preference materials and the PCGLOBE printouts, they analyze the region in terms of its geography, demography, economy and politics. They prepare a presentation outline for class distribution. I also prepare a critique sheet for students to use during each presentation to evaluate the speaker. When I post final grades, I also post each student's "audience rating."

Student outcomes from this combination of new resources and methods are very encouraging. Students learn to find and consider a wide new range of world news and opinions. They build an acceptance of statistical data and an interest in applying it analytically. They learn the major features of the world map, and the influence of geography on policy. They gain collaborative learning and presentation experience valuable for teaching and for most other work situations.

The final examination reflects the alternative methods and structure of the course. Students are given four PCGLOBE databases, one country from each region. Using comparative analysis, they must show how two of them do, or do not, prove the validity of one of the analytical themes. Their reaction to the exam form is overwhelmingly positive. Their papers have been thoughtful, analytical, and well documented.

The international press, as well as computerized maps and data bases, are typical products of

the information age. They especially animate contemporary history, promoting critical reading and thinking. Acquainting students with their pertinence and validity provides them with the tools to keep developing their global perspective. In particular, this approach shows prospective teachers the rewards of diversity and the richness of the resources available to them. These valuable media belong in the classroom.

Eleanor Turk
History
IU East

Communication

Giving Students Increased Responsibility for Learning Through Course Design and Inductive Approach

It is important that a student be given increased responsibility for his or her own learning. Students need to come to see that only they can learn for themselves and that they will not do so unless they actively and willingly engage themselves in the process.

In the past at IUK a majority of students registered for the basic public speaking course because it was required, participated in the course with apprehension and dread, and performed the assignments by memorizing the "rules" of public speaking. Their goal was simple: to "survive" the course. Most basic public speaking textbooks today appear adapted to these students' needs, providing them with a prescription for composing and delivering speeches, yet failing to convince them that the "art" that we call "speech" is valuable and that participating in "public conversation" is worthwhile.

During the past year, a colleague and I have grappled with and responded to these issues by redesigning the basic communication course at IUK and writing a workbook to accompany the course. We concluded that the most effective way of returning rhetoric to its status as an art was to place more of the responsibility for learning upon the students themselves. We adopted an inductive approach, whereby students read and heard dozens of professional and student speeches, analyzed those speeches at home, in small groups, and in class discussions, and derived principles of public speaking from a concrete understanding of their application. These principles were then applied in student speeches, which also became material for discussion. Teachers were responsible for ensuring that certain principles were discussed, that particular aspects of sample speeches were examined, and that students actively participated in this learning process by writing their own textbook, and listing their discoveries about the speeches in their workbook. By examining professional and student speeches, students are forced to consider under what circumstances speech "rules" might be followed or flouted in fulfilling particular speaking purposes. Such speeches need not be "model" speeches; much can be learned from rhetorical failures, as well as rhetorical successes.

The basic assumption guiding this approach is that speech is not merely a technique, a bag of tricks, or a means of persuasion, which can be learned by memorizing the "rules of public speaking." Instead, it is an art characterized by principles rather than rules. These principles cannot merely be memorized and followed; they must be understood as the significant considerations of people thinking and acting rhetorically. Rules either apply or they do not, although principles carry weight. It is much more difficult to teach students how to weigh principles against one another in a given situation than it is to note that one has followed or failed to follow a rule.

Susan Sciame-Giesecke
Speech Communication
IU Kokomo

Teachers were responsible for ensuring that certain principles were discussed, that particular aspects of sample speeches were examined, and that students actively participated in this learning process by writing their own textbook, and listing their discoveries about the speeches in their workbook.

Some Thoughts on Teaching Science

When preparing for a class (an interaction with my students about my discipline), I think about something I heard about teaching many years ago: TELLING IS NOT EQUAL TO TEACHING. How can I do something more than telling in my 50 minutes with my students?

We interact with, ask and sometimes answer questions about phenomena with which my discipline is concerned, and I attempt to be relevant.

I believe that the most successful scientists are those who are good at asking questions, yet my students get little experience at doing that. They get lots of chances to answer questions, and somehow we think that by doing this they will become good question askers. Some of them do poorly in my class because they can't predict what I will ask on the exam. They can't take the material which we have discussed and turn it into questions.

What to do???

The class needs to experience a phenomenon about which to ask questions. One such experience is to take a piece of paper about 8 1/2 inches by 1/2 inches. Have them tear it lengthwise about 1/3 of the away from one end. Then take the other end and fold it up about 1/2 inch. Place a paperclip on this folded end and then throw it up into the air. They discover they have made a whirlybird, a paper helicopter. Many questions can be generated and answers obtained by manipulating the variables of the whirlybird. Why does it work? What happens if I do this or that? Can I make it go clockwise or counterclockwise? Students are involved with their own creation. They have made something. It works. They have an investment in the learning process.

I'm sure every discipline has the discrepant event. In chemistry I can take pennies from 1983 and do something to them which makes them "float" on water. I then tell the class that they should ask me questions which are phrased so that the appropriate answer is either yes or no in order to try to find out why some of the pennies are "floating" on the water and other have sunk to the bottom.

Another way to get the students involved is to give a set of circumstances and ask what will happen if and why? Take a big, heavy object and ask students if it will float. Their experience is that big, heavy things don't float and they will be surprised when you show them that this particular one does. Ask, "Can a

handkerchief hold water in a glass when the glass of water is turned upside down?" Have the students vote. Have them take a stand, yes or no. They are then interested in checking out their ideas. They have a stake in the outcome, participating in their cognitive development.

Who are the heroes of your discipline? Can students replace some of their idols with some of yours? (Linus Pauling for Axl Rose, George Washington Carver for Eddie Murphy, whoever you can think of.)

Do your students ask questions of common things? For example, mylar balloons in the grocery store. Are they mylar? Some of the balloons are very complicated as I've discovered. The shiny stuff is aluminum, the underneath stuff is sometimes two layers thick, neither of which is mylar.

Think before you go to class:

1. Am I only prepared to tell?

2. Do I have any props?

3. What is the stuff of my discipline?

4. What are the questions of my discipline? Can I get my students to ask them?

5. Can I overcome with words the 4 H's that Luke Johnson suggested plague undergraduates: hungry, homesick, horny, or hungover? (FACET Lilly House, 1991).

6. How can I get them to participate in their own learning during the class, not just copying notes for later learning?

Art Friedel
Chemistry
IP Ft. Wayne

63

Writing

Guided Journal Writing as a First Step to Position Papers

Stimulating classroom teachers to approach their professional decision-making from a theoretical perspective is vital if we are to move teacher to meta-levels of thinking. To accomplish this goal, I have designed a research course which contains a number of elements that stimulate reflectivity about their practice and the profession.

One strategy is journal keeping: students write about some educational issue, success, failure, or concern in a daily log. They are given a template of questions to guide their analysis of the issue. Additionally, they are asked to pose three questions from each entry.

The journals become the source of inspiration for the primary requirement, which is writing a position paper on some educational issue that is of major importance to them. Guidelines are distributed to assist students in writing such a paper, often the first time they have been supported in writing in the first person. Most students value this requirement and have reported that they used the paper when interviewing for positions or writing philosophy of education statements.

I provide opportunities for students to submit drafts for my review and establish research teams to keep them moving forward and to provide critiques of each others' works. Some students resist this option, because of the time constrains it imposes and the tendency to work in a single burst of energy, rather than at stages throughout the course.

Finally, students present their works to the class for feedback, support and to provide other students' access to their emergent expertise. They delight in this opportunity, which also provides me with a major source of information regarding their intellectual growth.

Margo Sorgman
Social Studies
IU Kokomo

Four Stages of Essay Writing

The major challenge for me as a teacher is teaching students to write effectively. I require term papers or other written assignments in all of my courses. Each assignment is designed to be an integral part of the course. I have worked for many years to find the best approach for these writing assignments. It is a constant process of trial and error, and I depend on students to give me good feedback about what is helpful and what is not.

I structure the term paper assignment around four stages:

1. Initial Proposal   3. First Draft
2. Outline   4. Final Draft

For each of these steps I have developed a specific set of instructions and guidelines to help students. I return the assignment at each stage with constructive feedback as quickly as possible. I also provide students with the evaluation form I use to assess the paper so that they know the criteria on which the paper will be judged. While I am still in the process of refining my approach, I am able to see a qualitative difference in the papers students write. Written student evaluations also confirm the effectiveness of this approach.

Linda Gugin
Political Science
IU Southeast

Understanding Sources

In my introductory psychology course, I repeatedly found that students were unable to differentiate material heard on television or read in magazines from scientific inform-ation. Therefore, I assign the students three short (1 page) papers revolving around one topic. The topic may be anything to do with psychology, for example anorexia nervosa.

I repeatedly found that students were unable to differentiate material heard on television or read in magazines from scientific information.

In paper one, the student is required to use common forms of media (e.g., talk shows, magazines, newspapers).

In paper two, the student is required to summarize material from three scholarly journal articles.

In paper three, the student is required to compare and contrast the nature of the information found in the two types of sources.

In addition to developing better writing skills and learning how to find scholarly journal articles, the students have also demonstrated their greater understanding of "sources."

Robin Morgan
Psychology
IU Southeast

Viewing Term Papers as Process

In most of my lcasses, students are expected to write a term paper. Many students have not had sufficientexperience writing papers of this kind. In the past, I would have the paepr due at the end of the semester. Students who already knew how to write good papers did well; those who did not, didn't.

To discourage students from waiting until the end of the semester to get started, I began to require written and oral progress reports on their papers. I also offered a "re-write" option. Student swho turned in their papers well before the due date could benefit from my comments (which included commnts on writng style as well as substance), and turn the paper in again. I also offered to read portions of the final paper.

About one-third of the students take advantage of this option. Their papers improve dramatically, and they thank me for helping them learn how to write better.

Linda Haas
Sociology/Women's Studies
IUPUI

Responding to Student Papers
With Letters of Transmittal

A student wrote on her course evaluation that, as a writing teacher, I "should not be commenting on (her) ideas, but just marking mechanics, grammar, spelling, and punctuation." Once over my initial dismay at the above response, I realized that, had I known earlier of this student's discontent with my way of responding to her papers, we could have met to negotiate our different approaches to grading papers. As a consequence, I developed my version of a letter of transmittal to accompany each paper handed in for grading or for response. In this letter, students tell me what they hoped to accomplish in the paper, how they tried to accomplish this objective, what particular rhetorical strategies they used, whether any of these strategies were new or risky for them to try, what they feel good about in the paper, what they are concerned about in the paper, and what in particular they want me to focus upon in my response. Once they receive my response, they write me again or see me in conference, letting me know whether my response to their paper was helpful and meaningful.

I now feel guided through the students' papers by concerns they deem important, a significant step in helpnig students develop control over their learning. Grades seem less arbitrary and more closely related to mutually negotiated criteria. My responding is no longer a final pronouncement, but rather the middle state in an ongoing conversation about what and how my students are learning in my writing classes.

An example of a letter of transmittal follows:

Letter of Transmittal

Your letters will have three main sections: 1. Intentions
2. Process
3. The paper as product

Intentions: What you wanted to accomplish in this paper as a writer.

* For your reader
* In relation to the topic

Process: How you went about trying to accomplish your intentions.

* How your group influenced your writing.
* How your paper changed from draft to draft.
* What aspects of your writing you focused on most.

Paper as Product: How your paper matches your intentions.

* How well did you achieve your intentions?
* What do you feel especially satisfied with?
* What do you particularly want me to comment on?

Please feel free to tell me anything else about your paper that you think is important and that would help me read it in a manner most beneficial to you.

Two cautions:

Please do not write that this paper is not for any particular audience and that you just needed to write the paper to explore the topic for yourself. Although that is indeed a legitimate function of writing, it is not the nature of writing that this course is about. You are to find meaning in your personal situation or viewpoint that will have interest or significance for others as well as for yourself.

Please do not write a blanket request saying that you want me to comment generally on anything that concerns me. I will do that automatically. My purpose in asking you to focus my response is to show me how aware you already are of your writing strengths and needs, and how this awareness changes or develops as the semester progresses.

(These letters are usually 1-2 pages in length, and are typed in letter format.)

Sharon Hamilton
English
IUPUI

Readers Theater Approach to Expository Writing

Assigning tasks in graduate education classes that will encourage students to explore an issue that they deem important by drawing upon current theoretical and pedagogical literature and applying it to their own teaching contexts. In particular, I want to avoid unquestioning adherence to one philosophical approach or the establishment of reductive dichotomies.

I introduce my students to a dialogic readers theater approach to expository writing. They conduct their research - primary and secondary - as usual. However, in writing up their research, they pay attention to dissenting and dissonant voices by creating personae who exemplify different perspectives on the issue or concept they are exploring. The resulting paper, in script format, is performed by members of the class, and then responded to with questions and discussion.

Students who are just encountering new ideas are not forced into playing the role of "pseudo-expert" often thrust upon them by their traditional view of an expository research-based paper. Their papers demonstrate the dilemmas they face, and allow them to see why others might hold viewpoints quite different from theirs and consider them equally valid. In fact, one student recently said, "Now I understand why Mrs. Hardwick is so resistant to new ideas. She's scared. She's learned how to copy by using tried-and-true methods, and is afraid that if she tries something new, she'll lose control." That kind of understanding is crucial for teachers working with colleagues in the same school or department.

Equally exciting was the discovery one student made that, "All of these characters are really me. Sometimes I think this is the way to respond to student writing; other times, I just want to get rid of all those mechanical errors; sometimes I just want to sit down and cry and give it all up. All of these people are me, but now I understand how they all relate to each other in the way that I respond to my students' writing."

Sharon Hamilton
English
IUPUI

Sequenced Short Writing Assignments in Business Law

The teaching challenges I have faced in the recent past have centered around my efforts to learn to use writing assignments to foster mastery of course material and to give students practice in making their thoughts visible through the written word.

I have devised weekly writing assignments for my introductory business law course (honors and intensive writing versions only) which are sequenced in terms of type and difficulty of task and which force students to analyze factual situations and apply legal concepts and rules to those facts in order to come up with a defensible solution to a legal problem.

This has proved to me that writing in a course need not be some enormous lengthy paper that comes in at the end of the semester and which students never see again, and that writing really does help students master difficult material and learn to work critically through it. I have not yet mastered "minimal marking," a method of marking students' papers which is brief and fast. I still feel compelled to write paragraphs of red ink on my students' papers, and to do much of the rethink and editing which I should leave to them.

Laura Ginger
Business Law
IU Bloomington

Four-Section Journal

I ask students to turn in a "journal" after each week of an introductory class. Students get format instructions on their course syllabi, followed by explanations and descriptive examples during the first class. Each journal has four sections with instructions that go something like this:

1. Describe our class as a group. What single activity did the group seem to enjoy most this week? What was the interest level, activity level, and mood of the group? How did these vary during the week?

2. Describe your own reaction to the above items. If your reaction is similar to the group's, share your perspective or insight about your favorite week's activity.

3. Describe two classmates, either singly or in interaction. Tell me what you heard them say or do to attract your attention, then report your interpretation of those events.

4. How might you apply a concept from this week's class to your life? Be specific ('Learning is a wonderful thing' has been used before). Tell me what you found useful and where or when you might employ your knowledge.

Journals are graded with a check plus, check, or check minus indicating the extent to which the student follows the format. Content is not graded; my responses, jokes, retorts, and musings create a dialogue with each person.

Soon, students routinely earn a check plus on each journal and begin to focus on our dialogue instead of on earning grades. My written comments are not intended to evaluate ideas, but to expand on something the student writes or to point out a similar new concept.

Sometimes students ask for specific answers to their questions and I respond by explaining and clarifying. Most of my comments involve encouragement and validation.

Although the journals involve several hours each week for responses (which is sometimes tiring), at the conclusion of each semester I suddenly find myself missing the correspondence.

The journal format reinforces observation skills taught in the class. The journals also provide continuous feedback on student likes and dislikes, revealing how easily students comprehend material in order to apply it. Most importantly, the journals provide a dialogue between student and teacher that affects the climate of our work together.

George Leddick
Counselor Education
IP Ft. Wayne

Science Writing

I teach an advanced laboratory course in molecular genetics, and require my students to write two formal lab reports in journalism article style. I treat their reports as though they were manuscripts to be submitted from my own research laboratory, and I critique them accordingly. I then meet with each student to discuss the report. Students then revise the reports before turning them in for a grade.

I treat their reports as though they were manuscripts to be submitted from my own research laboratory, and I critique them accordingly.

Most students submit two or more drafts for critiquing before they submit a version for grading, and I critique each draft. My students frequently comment that they have never had this experience in a course before, and the improvement in their writing is often dramatic, and always substantial. I also encourage my students to review one another's reports, and assign "peer review partners" for this purpose. This is especially effective for the second lab report, when students have already had some experience with science writing, and have more of an appreciation for this specialized skill.

Mimi Zolan
Biology
IU Bloomington

What is a Dialogue Journal?

A dialogue journal is a rich merger of personal and public writing. As with most journals, writers express their thoughts about a reading, a discussion, a lecture, or an experience.

If we believe that knowledge is socially constructed, that writing aids discovery of ideas and beliefs, and we all need to communicate our ideas, we may choose the dialogue journal as one way to support creation of knowledge, discovery and affirmation of learning, and communication of ideas.

The purpose of the journal entry:

✎ **To discover what the writer thinks about a topic.**

✎ **To brainstorm possible sources of information.**

✎ **To consider pros and cons of a position.**

✎ **To raise questions about an assigned reading.**

✎ **To complain about confusion.**

✎ **To wonder among many thoughts.**

✎ **To generate a record of a thought process.**

Journals are often used in classes as a site for personal writing. Sometimes the journals are read by others, but they are not primarily used for communication with others.

A dialogue journal, however, also has conversation as part of its purpose. In this variety of journal, writers still express their own thoughts, but know they will have the opportunity for response. Someone else will read the journal entry and write a reaction to the ideas there.

Dialogue journals are organized so that different ideas exist side-by-side for reflection and analysis.

> **Writers draw a vertical line down the page about three-fourths of the way across.**
>
> **The journal's owner writes in the left-hand three-fourths of the page.**
>
> **The responder writes in the right-hand one-fourth of the page.**
>
> **Each writer dates the entry.**
>
> **The responder signs his or her name so the writer can initiate more conversation.**

Using Dialogue Journals

Dialogue journals may be used in a number of ways:

1. The writer enters questions as she reads her textbook. At the beginning of class another student reads the questions and writes answers or amplifications of the questions to ask aloud later in class.

2. The writer enters notes from his textbook reading. As he listens to a lecture, he augments points in his journal with points from the lecture. His own notes on both sources of information show similarities or differences. If the lecture comes before the reading, the student takes notes in the left column as he listens.

After he reads, in the right column he adds only new information or ideas, either from the book or from his own synthesis of lecture and book ideas. The conversation is within the writer's mind, engaged by a text, a lecture, and his own thoughts.

3. After a class discussion, the student has five minutes to write about the most interesting (most confusing, most important, most controversial) point in the discussion. For added points, another student has five minutes to respond with clarification, further questions, disagreement, or reflection. The journal owner then reads and may jot responses under the other student's comments. If time allows, students may talk together about their entries.

4. A class period begins with each student writing a journal entry in response to a focus question posed by the teacher. Then another student is asked to play the believing game or the doubting game: either the student supports the writer's answer with further evidence, confirmation of reasoning, or personal testimony; or, the student refutes the writer's answer with contradictory evidence, debate about reasoning, or contrary experience. After the writer has the opportunity to read the response, the class discussion for the day begins with students focused and thinking.

5. At home, students write in their dialogue journals about possible topics for papers.

In class, two classmates respond to the ideas, focusing on what would interest them as readers; or what seems appropriate for course or assignment goals; or on the ease or difficulty of finding topic sources. For the next class, students narrow their topic selections to two. This time a classmate responds with advice about which topic seems most feasible for this writer.

6. At the beginning of the semester, students define a term or situation, or take a stand on a topic. At points throughout the semester they return to the initial journal entry to affirm or change their minds in the response column. At semester's end they make another journal entry which includes the results of all their thinking about the topic throughout the semester, easily traceable through their journal entries.

Communal Dialogue Journals

A class has a communal dialogue journal. Kept on the edge of a desk or table, it is available for entries and responses by class members.

1. A student may express confusion about an assignment; another student or the faculty member may explain.

2. A student may announce a television program about course content; a viewer may later share an important point in the response column.

3. A student may ask for a volunteer reader of a paper draft; a classmate may offer to be a reader or may defer this time but be available another.

This dialogue journal is invaluable in a large class, useful in a small one, and helpful in both for understanding the progress of learning.

Barbara Cambridge
English/Campus Writing
IUPUI

Term Paper Workshops

Each semester in all my graduate and upper-level undergraduate classes, I assign a term paper varying in length from 15-30 pages. For over a decade, I also have required a discrete set of steps, culminating in the final version of the paper itself. For example, within the first month of the semester, the graduate students provide me with:

* **Note cards**

* **A detailed outline of the paper as they currently envision it**

* **Photocopies of the literature consulted**

After making written comments on this work (sometimes coupled with a student conference), I require a full-blown rough draft, including documentation and bibliography, due a month later.

Although I take into account the vagaries of the individual student's schedules and allow some latitude, I urge the students to meet this deadline in a timely fashion. I then criticize the rough draft and include a checklist that sets out the most common substantive (e.g., insufficient documentation) and non-substantive (e.g., tense shifts or ineffective transitions) errors.

Students have three to four weeks for revision before turning in the final version (as well as all prior drafts, checklists, comments, and photocopies of research).

This regime has worked well for the following reasons:

1. **It spurs the students into commencing their papers at a much earlier date, thus assuring a more polished final product.**

2. **Diffuseness, insufficient research, inadvertent plagiarism, egregious stylistic errors, and similar problems surface earlier and become more readily remediable.**

3. **In addition to individual learning, this process invites collaborative learning as well.**

To reinforce this objective of the assignment, I show the students my own heavily-marked articles-in-process. When the students see that I concurrently am experiencing frustrations that parallel their own, the purposefulness born of a mutual goal - the improvement of our respective research efforts - cause the proprietariness and defensiveness criticism reaction to dissipate.

Last and most important, the paper quality rises dramatically, a "plus" for me because of time spent grading the final versions, and for the students, because of the grade earned and overall personal satisfaction.

While my belief in their regime weathers the criticisms of its few detractors (who sometimes mistake my zeal for high quality and my emphasis on critical thinking as obsessiveness), it clearly involves a substantial investment of my time. In addition to the mandatory rough draft, I offer to criticize <u>all</u> the drafts the students undertake. Many of the 35-40 students therefore opt to complete two or three rough drafts. My resolve to continue this approach despite these demands on my time derives from the students' recognition of their improvement and the opportunity this gives me, an avowed advocate of "writing across the curriculum," to illustrate the relationship between lucidity of expression and clarity of thinking.

I show the students my own heavily-marked articles-in-process. When the students see that I concurrently am experiencing frustrations that parallel their own, the purposefulness born of a mutual goal - the improvement of our respective research efforts - cause the proprietariness and defensiveness criticism reaction to dissipate.

By semester's end, the students are convinced that clear writing and clear thinking are wedded. They also realize that they have appreciably enhanced their skills in these two vital areas and confidently carry over these (sometimes hard-won) capabilities to their future courses.

Brenda Knowles
Business Law
IU South Bend

Colllaborating on Defining Good Writing

Teaching Context:

It is the beginning of a semester. Students do not know each other very well, nor can I assume that they have a common or shared metadiscourse to talk about their writing. This following activity helps them to get to know each other while simultaneously establishing common values and understanding about what constitutes good writing.

Strategy:

1. Each student lists <u>five qualities</u> of what constitutes "good writing."

2. In pairs, students agree upon a common list of <u>six qualities</u> of "good writing."

3. Each pair finds another pair, and agree upon a common list of <u>seven qualities</u> of "good writing."

4. Each group of four finds another group of four, and agree upon a common list of <u>eight qualities</u> of "good writing."

By this time, the class is generally in two large groups. Each group sends a representative to write its list on the board, and we compare lists as a whole class. Since, during the negotiations, someone may have had to give up an aspect of good writing that he or she felt to be important, an opportunity is given at this time to get it back into the list. Also, in comparing the two lists, as well as during the prior negotiations and discussions, students can see which of several ways of expressing similar concepts might be more effective. although the exercise takes almost a whole class period, a considerable amount of talk about writing has been done by students as they get to know each other socially and intellectually.

I then take the final list approved by the class and arrange it interestingly on a page, type it up, and distribute it to the whole class as their agreed upon views of writing by which to consider the writing they will do throughout the semester. I have attached a sample from one of my advanced expository writing classes:

Sharon Hamilton
English
IUPUI

Our Class Statement of
"Good Writing"

Good Writing

    flows smoothly

    moves coherently from one idea to another

        is organized according to ideas and intentions

conveys the writer's vision to readers

     understandably and interestingly

elaborates appropriately to develop

message/point/focus/stance/thesis/purpose

       with appropriate

mechanics

        invites reading

lingers in the memory

    is honest, sincere, authentic,

sparks personal meaning; stimulates feeling and/or thought

has something that sets it apart, above the mundane.

    alive   fresh

        playful   surprising

         unique   has impact!

EXAMS

The Contract:
A Solution to the End-of-the-Semester Student Panic

Because I (and most faculty) clearly explain the procedure for totaling final grades on the syllabus, any student could derive the final grade or come close to it without last-minute office hour visits. However, after two or three semesters of addressing these questions, it was clear to me that students are really there for a number of other reasons and, by accident, I hit on "The Contract." **This solution is based on the idea that what students really want in these panicked meetings is two fold: motivation and social support.** In fact, it takes very little to provide these.

Towards the end of each semester, I get a stack of brightly colored paper that I put on a corner of my desk. When a student comes in with the question: "What am I going to get in this course?," I take out my grade book and one of the sheets of paper. I then write the student's name in large letters at the top of the paper and underneath, write their grades to date. Then, I ask them what they think is the best they can offer me, and what they think they might get, etc. on the final (depending on the nature of the conversation to that point). I write that down and simply figure out the grade. In my classes, I offer some incentive for improvement over the semester and vary the assignments, but to show a simple case where there are three equally weighted exams:

Exam I	Exam II
B (85)	B+ (88)

Expect Exam III	Final Grade
A (95)	89.3 = A-

Given the improvement, I tell them that I would jump them to an A-. I then sign the contract and ask them to do the same. I tell them that this is a binding contract and if they do as they say they will, they will get the A-. If that does not happen, they can show me their contract which I will keep on the same corner of my desk for one semester. This is no different from what I would have done under the stated grading policy but it seems to work quite well in allaying student anxiety.

Often, I will work through a number of scenarios with students if they wish, (e.g., offering different final exam possible outcomes) or start from a different point. If a student comes in and says "What do I have to do in this class to pass, get an A, etc.? " I simply sit down and figure it out with them, write a contract and sign it. Again, it does not change the outcome of the course grade but does seem to influence their feelings about attaining that higher final exam grade.

Marilyn Watkins
Education
IU East

Relieving Test Anxiety

Test anxiety tends to torment older students the worst as they face fears of returning to school after a long absence. I have found a few techniques that lessen their uneasiness:

I use colored paper for my tests instead of white paper.

I include cartoons at various places in the exam.

I put Daffy Duck or some other character on the front cover.

These highlights take a bit of the seriousness out of the occasion.
To lessen the severity of losing points:

I grade with a green pen instead of red. I use this to emphasize that their errors are corrections rather than failures.

For all students who received a D or F on the first exam, I write a note asking them to make an appointment. This gives me the opportunity to counsel them about studying tactics. By forcing them to come to my office, I lessen their fears about approaching me for help. After a few minutes of discussion, we _both_ find we are human beings which makes any return trips for help easier. The purpose is not to make them defend their score but to see what _we_ can do to improve their performance. Plus, students get the chance to unload about problems they may be having. This also lets students know I am not judging them.

Students with poor test scores often feel they have let me down, think I don't like them, or think they're dumb. Once I dispel those feelings, they work harder. Whether to prove themselves or to please me, their performance improves, albeit in some cases only marginally.

Because of the number of students and the demands on my time, I limit the time of each conference to about 15 minutes. By scheduling students in clusters, they know someone is waiting to see me which speeds up the process. Fifteen minutes is enough time to accomplish my goal and avoids repetition.

Katherine Phelps
Finance
South Bend

Authentic Gratitude

In my undergraduate classes in which the students write several short papers throughout the semester, I respond differently to the last paper that I grade. This paper is usually due about three weeks before the semester ends. In addition to the standard feedback that I write in the margins and at the ends of papers about thesis quality, evidence, logic of the arguments, and styllistics, I write additional messages. For each student, I write several sentences about what I have especially appreciated in their contributions to class.

For each student, I write several sentences about what I have especially appreciated in their contributions to class.

For some students, I write about the ways their discussion comments have shown real-life applications of theory. For others, I recognize the value of their keen listening skills. To some I write "thanks" for their after-class comments and participation. This allows me to express authentic gratitude, to personalize the last assignment, and to reinforce good class participation habits. Students, as you might expect, are surprised and pleased with the notes.

Jo Young Switzer
Communication
IU Ft. Wayne

✓ ✗ ✓ ✗

Imagination In Context

Students often fear essay examinations and seek the easy path to success by regurgitating as much of the lectures as they can recall. In order to make this as unlikely as possible, I strive to invent imaginative questions which call upon students to place themselves in a particular historical situation and write an essay making use of what they have learned from readings and lectures. There is no single or obviously correct answer, and they are graded on their writing, their imagination, and their accurate use of the historical context. I always offer a choice of questions, and many students select the more traditional type.

These sample questions are all taken from Indiana History, an upper division course without prerequisites which attracts many non-majors:

I strive to invent imaginative questions which call upon students to place themselves in a particular historical situation and write an essay making use of what they have learned from readings and lectures.

---

1. Imagine yourself in the position of Captain Thomas Harper of the First Infantry, stationed in Fort Wayne early in 1815. The war is drawing to a close and you have decided to leave the army to settle in the Indiana Territory where you have been stationed for the past four years. Write a letter to your beloved Sally Carroll persuading her to accept your previous proposal of marriage, even though it will mean living on the frontier instead of the civilized city of Baltimore.
Or:
Imagine yourself in the position of Sally Carroll and explain why you cannot bring yourself to live on the frontier even though it means breaking your engagement.
(Interestingly, both men and women selected both versions of the question. Some wrote believable love letters, others submitted an examination-style answer weakly disguised as a letter.)

2. "The Calumet Region is legally part of Indiana, but culturally it is a world apart. It cannot legitimately be considered 'Hoosier' and ought to be given to Chicago."

Comment, thoughtfully, considering both the view from Indianapolis and the interests of the residents of "da region."

3. Was the Ku Klux Klan merely an aberration or perversion of the early 1920's, or did it give visible manifestation of deep-seated Hoosier attitudes which both antedated and survived the klan itself?

4. Suppose yourself a young Indianapolis lawyer sent to California in 1847 to obtain the signature of George Amberson Minafer on a deed required to clear the title to three lots in the Amberson Addition. What might he tell you about his family, his own life, and life in Indianapolis when he lived there as a boy and young man? Hint: Use your own imagination as well as your historical hindsight to go beyond what Booth Tarkington wrote in The Magnificent Ambersons or what Orson Welles dramatized in the film version.

5. Describe and contrast the normal routines of daily life during the 1880's for one of the following pairs of Hoosier residents:

A. A farm boy from the southern Indiana hills and the son of an Indianapolis banker, both aged 16 or 17.

B. A LaPorte County farm wife and the wife of a moderately successful lawyer in Crawfordsville, both of an age between 35 and 45.

C. A black resident of Indianapolis and a recent immigrant from Italy living in Mishawaka, either male or female and in their late teens or early twenties.

D. Explicate and defend the poetry of James Whitcomb Riley.

(I have used this last question twice, without finding a student with the nerve to attempt it, but the exam offers several other choices. Personally I find Riley almost impossible to read, but I try not to let students know this. Many have heard him praised as Indiana's greatest poet, but in the northern part of the state he is admired in the abstract and unread in actuality.)

Patrick Furlong
History
IU South Bend

Discussing Tests

The absolute worst days are when you hand back the exams. The atmosphere of hostility is palpable and is usually accompanied by murmuring and veiled comments about your ancestry. Sometimes lynch mobs gather near your office or marauding students, armed with pitchforks and torches, wait for you in the parking lot.

Well, maybe it's not all that bad, but the uneasy undercurrent on those days is, at the very least, distracting. How do you deal with this hostility? I've found one effective method. On the day that I hand back the test, I declare yet another rule:

As a human being, you have a right to make mistakes. As a student, you have an obligation to learn from them.

As a result, I do not discuss the tests on the day I return them. I do not answer any questions about material covered by the exam. I claim that I have been discussing this material for several weeks already. Think of the delay as a "cooling off" period. Stick to your guns. Some students will try to ask you privately for answers. Don't give in.

I do, however, promise to answer any substantive questions about the test during the next class period. Of course, if there has been an arithmetic error (not a partial credit quibble), I will correct it immediately.

I do offer advice to the woebegone by suggesting that they not get mad at me or themselves, but instead sit down with their notes and texts to figure out what they did wrong. I didn't take that test, they did. They're responsible for the results. After all, recognizing a mistake is as important as correcting it.

Believe it or not, this delay tactic does quell some of the class anger and petulance. If nothing else, by the next class, they are less emotional about the exam and my responses to questions then become more of a review than an apology. The stalling also minimizes nitpicking about partial credit and subjective grading.

Another advantage? The day I hand back the tests is not a lost class period. I start a new lecture. If some of the new material has a connection with test questions, I don't shy away from it, but do make obvious hints about the connections.

Bill Frederick
Computer Science
Ft. Wayne

"The atmosphere of hostility is palpable and is usually accompanied by murmuring and veiled comments about your ancestry. Sometimes lynch mobs gather near your office or marauding students, armed with pitchforks and torches, wait for you in the parking lot.

Well, maybe it's not all that bad..."

TEACHING NON-TRADITIONAL ADULT LEARNERS

Remaining Flexible With Students' Personal Commitments

The vast majority of graduate students taking my classes are professionals working full-time, often in lower management positions. In addition, they have family and community obligations that require time and effort. A recurring problem for both the students and myself is their need to miss classes due to professional or personal commitments beyond their control. I have attempted to solve the problem by remaining as flexible as possible regarding assignments and examination dates; and also by developing resources that will allow the student to obtain the essence of the class experience outside regularly scheduled class times.

I have attempted to make it possible for students who must miss class to remain on a knowledge acquisition level with their peers, so that they will not be disadvantaged when they must meet commitments outside of class.

---

1. Students may schedule exams at times that are more accessible to them as long as appropriate proctors are available.

2. I maintain a library of video tapes of my classes which students may check out and view at home.

3. I allow students to audiotape the classes, and will operate the student's recorders myself if the student can't be in class. My only requirement is that the student provide the equipment and that the tapes be 90 minutes long, the length of the class.

4. I give students my home phone and encourage them to call me if they have questions.

5. I have constructed a notebook for students which follows the lectures. All visual materials and class examples are reproduced in the notebook and available to all students. This allows the student who hasn't been personally in class to pull the material together.

6. Student's work is graded by means of T-scores; therefore, their grades are dependent upon how well they perform when compared to their peers.

I have attempted to make it possible for students who must miss class to remain on a knowledge acquisition level with their peers, so that they will not be disadvantaged when they must meet commitments outside of class.

Juanita Keck
Nursing
IUPUI

A Sense of Humor

Using Cartoons

One of my students once did a study correlating the ratings of cartoon humor with the subject's knowledge of the topic represented in the cartoon. As you might expect, he found that people without adequate knowledge did not find the cartoon funny. Developmental studies of humor suggest that something is funny when you are no longer struggling with the task or concept. It is this interrelationship between humor and knowledge (as well as my appreciation of an instructor with a good wit) that has led me to intentionally integrate humor into my classes.

Humor is not only intimately connected with understanding, it is also pleasurable.

Laughing makes people feel good. For many students, college courses do not contain much to feel good about. The material is difficult, the concepts serious, and often the presentation of the material promotes boredom more often than any pleasurable emotion.

One of my course goals is to help students understand the humor related to course content and have more pleasurable experiences as they experience their own competence. I also encourage them to deal with ordinary life experiences as stimulus for thoughtful examination. I do this in several ways:

I often use cartoons or humorous anecdotes as introductions to lectures. If the students have read the material, they are immediately amused as well as having the positive feeling associated with understanding something. I feel they are more receptive to learning and more likely to attend to the material than when they hear words that just repeat what they have read in the book. If they do not understand the concept, the cartoon provides me with an opportunity to explain the concept illustrated. (Egocentrism in the young child is illus- trated in a Family Circle cartoon by Bill Keane. A child is talking on the phone while playing with a yo-yo. The caption reads "Look what I can do, Grandma.")

I use cartoons that relate to concepts discussed in earlier classes as the basis for pop quizzes or exam questions. A cartoon is a little less threatening than a complex essay question, but the student must identify the concept illustrated and explain the relevant information. (A lecture on instinct and imprinting that discusses Konrad Lorenz and his experience with imprinting in ducks is tested with a quiz which presents a Gary Larson cartoon of a scientific looking man in a white coat following a line of ducks across a road. The caption reads, "When imprinting studies go awry." The question: Name the researcher and describe the research that is suggested by this cartoon.) I have stopped inserting humorous but related answers as options in multiple choice questions. This appears to confuse students who are anxious about exams and having difficulty with the material.

I occasionally draw cartoons on the board (and not very well, I might add) that relate to concepts currently under discussion. For example, cat and dog shaped animals are drawn to discuss the development of a concept which differentiates between cats and dogs.

I use puns, plays on words, or other verbal humor to increase attention to concepts and to facilitate memory. For example, if the left side of the brain is dominant in right handed people, and the right side of the brain is dominant in left handed people; then only left handed people are in their right minds.

Legitimizing humor as part of learning encourages the student to apply concepts learned in class to outside experiences. Students frequently report understanding a joke in a TV show or bring in cartoons that they feel illustrate a point we have discussed. I am assured that they know the content, because they understand the joke and find it funny.

Susan Shapiro
Psychology
IU East

Mistakes on the Board

As hard as I try to avoid doing so, I often make mistakes when copying material on the blackboard. Hopefully, one or more of my students will point out my mistake. The first time this happens during a course, I thank the student and tell a story about a person I greatly admire - my favorite teacher, Professor Steve Worland of Notre Dame. Steve was the most enthusiastic teacher I have ever known. He was a dynamo and his mind was so quick that, like a chess player, his thoughts were several moves ahead of his fingers and chalk. This quickness caused him to make lots of mistakes on the board! One day, when discussing Marx's labor theory

> **Students make mistakes, teachers make mistakes, we are all human, and we need to help each other get through this course.**

of value, he mislabeled the supply and demand curves in the traditional economics graph. None of us students mentioned the problem. Nevertheless, with eyes glazed over, Steve proceeded to rewrite everything he ever knew about Marx's theory to conform to his mistaken graph. We were all

sure that after class he went back to his office to wonder about this strange turn of events.

After telling the story, I acknowledge my fault again, and ask my students to let me know when I have made mistakes, since I am not nearly the teacher Steve Worland was, particularly in terms of his quickness and ingenuity.

Moral: Students make mistakes, teachers make mistakes, we are all human, and we need to help each other get through this course.

John Peck
Economics
IU South Bend

Feedback or Criticism?

Sometimes students seem unusually "weired" before a class begins.

Class Conduct

First, listen , and listen respectfully.

Disrespect . . . is embarrassing and puts you "on the spot."

Feedback or Criticism?

What do you do with the occasional student who, despite your best efforts to provide clear standards for work and effective feedback, doesn't hear what you are trying to say? With the student who cannot accept criticism, even constructive criticism that has been coupled with recognition of what he had done well? With the student who charges into your office, furious about written feedback which she regards as unjust, or else undone by comments that she sees as finishing off any hope she ever had about succeeding in the career she has chosen?

Most of us face criticism in life. Most of us also find it difficult to hear what we don't want to hear, but may __need__ to hear. Hearing so we can benefit from the observations and insights with which we are presented is an important life skill to acquire. And better now, in the relative safety of the college environment, than later, in the work place.

Over the years, I have learned some simple ways to work with such students. One is a skill I learned in a parenting class:

1. First, listen, and listen respectfully; the student may have insights that you need to hear.

2. When the student has finished saying what's on her mind, repeat what you think you hear her saying.

3. Silently consider the student's comments, and modify your discussion of her work, as needed.

4. When you are finished, ask the student to repeat back what she heard you saying.

5. Correct any misunderstandings.

6. Listen again, if you need to, and repeat the process as often as needed to arrive at mutual understanding.

If the student still does not hear what you are trying to say, you may need to do more:

1. First, ask the student Have you ever responded in this way to feedback before?

2. Rush to say the student doesn't need to tell you; she simply needs to think about the question. For herself.

3. If the student can honestly say (to herself) that she has never had this response before, then maybe there is something about the kind of feedback you are providing that is different from what she has experienced before, and that is worth both of you understanding. On the other hand, if the student has had this response before (remember, she doesn't have to tell you), then maybe there is something else going on - within her - that she would do well to examine.

Most of us face criticism in life. Most of us also find it difficult to hear what we don't want to hear, but may need to hear. Hearing so we can benefit from the observations and insights with which we are presented is an important life skill to acquire. And better now, in the relative safety of the college environment, than later, in the work place. Convey that to your student, and perhaps share some of your own difficulties in learning how to hear what you didn't want, but needed to know about your work. Let the student know you are on her side. Remind her that you simply want her to be the best she can be, and you will be there for her, not only providing her with your own insights concerning her work, but also, helping her, if she needs it, to work through the discomfort of receiving those insights.

In my experience, listening actively and discussing the challenges of receiving criticism are usually all it takes for students to begin to listen to what you have to say and get on with the business of learning.

Holly Stocking
Journalism
IU Bloomington

Classroom Conflict

When conflict arises in class, regardless of whether it is between student and teacher or student and student, there is an effective means of dealing with the problem. The key is to remember: description should come before evaluation. That is, simply get all parties involved to agree on what happened before any judgements are rendered. Despite how well we think human beings communicate, it is surprising that most conflicts are merely mis-communication. As a consequence, it does little good to discuss (read "argue") until all involved agree on what actually occurred (read "have a common basis for discussion").

Axiomatic to this rule is that all parties involved in such a grievance have basic rights of respect and privacy. So, any real deliberations should occur privately with only the involved parties. The class should not act as a jury. It is part of teacher responsibility to keep such conflicts from interfering with the pedagogical imperative. Discussion and arbitrations should be deferred until after class, if possible.

Description should come before evaluation. That is, simply get all parties involved to agree on what happened before any judgements are rendered.

I have been practicing this method for fifteen years and find it very effective. Indeed, most conflicts can be resolved quite simply once all agree on the actual events.

Warning: do not try this at home. Practicing psychological ploys and artifices can damage your personal relationships.

Bill Frederick
Computer Science
IP Ft. Wayne

Student Behavior

I tell my colleagues that the best way to avoid having to discipline misbehaving students is to not have any students who misbehave. While such advice may, on first blush, appear to be tongue-in-cheek, there really is a strong element of truth in that statement.

Sooner or later, we will all face the terror of confrontation with a misbehaving student. Whether such errant behavior involves unruliness or disrespect is less a matter of concern than is our ability to handle the behavior correctly.

To earn student respect we must deal with behavioral problems - as unpleasant as this may be. Our ability to deal with the problem is really a question of leadership. Being a tyrant is not the answer; neither is being too permissive.

Our ability to deal with the problem is really a question of leadership.

Unruly conduct or rowdiness is the easiest type of behavioral problem to control. Sometimes students seem unusually "weird" before a class begins. Thus, getting the class's collective attention is difficult. Starting the lecture as if you were oblivious to the din is improper. You are also punishing the quiet students. In such cases, I have often started a written dialogue discussion. That is, requesting that for about two minutes, students jot down any thoughts prompted by some open-ended, yet thought provoking phrase (such as **Ideas die hard** or **Changing of the Guard**). This is a good way for everyone to settle down without your appearing to demand order. At the same time, you have not really started your lecture; thus, none of your students have missed any vital material.

Disrespect, whatever form it takes, is embarrassing and puts you "on the spot." Try to meet the student afterward to discuss the problem. The student was wrong but certainly can be forgiven. Many instances of disrespect spring from momentary anger and frustration.

Discipline is each professor's responsibility. Proper administration of it will lead to improved effectiveness in the conduct of your classes.

Robert H. Orr
Computer Technology
IUPUI

Critical Incidents:

Relating Intergroup Conflict to Race and Culture

"Critical incidents" are written by my students during their school practicum. Students are asked to describe a situation (positive or negative) that stands out in their minds, or that seems puzzling or disturbing. These incidents are discussed in class.

A critical incident occurred in my own class, a multicultural education seminar that accompanies the school practicum. I decided to write it up and use it as a springboard for strengthening the students' decision making skills and for working toward resolution of the conflict.

Critical Incident in S503, a teacher decision-making simulation:

About half-way through the African-American group presentation one member of this class (we'll call her Denise) expressed her concerns about our group and the way the course was progressing. She stated that she felt isolated, uncomfortable, unheard and unaccepted. Since this course is about multicultural education, Denise stated that we were not achieving our goal of comfortable human relations among ourselves, let alone in ethnically-diverse schools. She questioned how effective many of the white students would be as teachers of black students. She also stated that the class didn't interact much with her because she is black. Another black woman in our class (we'll call her Maya) supported Denise's position. She added that she represented the program's 15% quota for minorities (no such quota exists).

As teacher I decided to pursue the discussion even though this meant the African-American group could not finish their presentation. Just before class ended I asked everyone to write to me about their feelings regarding what had happened in class. Most of the students wrote that they respected Denise for expressing her thoughts and feelings. Some had been aware that tensions were brewing and that they had felt uncomfortable too. Most (possibly all) of the white students expressed dismay, even anger, over the accusation that they were racist. A number stated that they disliked some of the behaviors displayed by Maya, behaviors they perceived to be rude, aggressive and

even racist. Some felt it was difficult to approach Denise because she seemed rigid, cold and negative toward whites. Several of the white students stated that they are personally shy and are slow to approach any new acquaintance.

As the teacher who has heard these opinions, seen the behaviors and read the journals, I wonder how much of this is due to the various perspectives and assumptions the students hold. I also wonder to what extent phenomena are due to feelings of insecurity, personality traits, or stage of ethnicity various perspectives and assumptions the students hold. I also wonder to what extent the phenomena are due to feelings of insecurity, personality traits, or stage of ethnicity evolution? How do Maya and Denise perceive others in the class? What cues are they tuning into and what assumptions are they making?

During the following class meeting I shared the major themes that had emerged in the students' written comments. I asked Denise if she wished to express any additional concerns and she declined. Then I asked the class as a whole, and again no response. Given the fact that I allowed no wait time, I wonder if the white students in class were given sufficient voice.

Over a month has passed and class has not met during the practicum period, Yet, as I visit the various schools I feel that the tensions are still brewing. I don't want to beat a dead horse, or accuse undue pain for any of my students, but I also don't want to sweep this under the rug. I suggest the following process to address the issue.

Procedure:

Students meet in small groups based on their research teams.

Instructor distributes the critical incident scenario and reads it aloud as the students follow.

Each team completes the decision making sheet (shown on next page) and reports to the class.

DECISION MAKING SHEET

Step 1:   Identify the major problem(s) to be solved.

Step 2:   Assume that you are the teacher who must decide what to do with this class. State your major values and goals (approximately 3-5 of each).

Step 3:   Brainstorm and list all possible actions you could take as the teacher of this class.

Step 4:   For each alternative, identify the possible consequences and place them in positive/negative categories.

Step 5:   Select the best course of action and justify your decision.

Step 6:   Present your identification of the problem, decision and your justification in class.

Step 7:   Individually write a brief explanation of your feelings about your decision and the process you went through.

Step 8:   Individually or in groups, write one or more follow-up questions for class discussion.

Christine Bennett
Multicultural Education
IU Bloomington

ELECTRONIC

CLASSROOM

Electronic Conversation

Based on her very successful experience in a course this summer, a student encouraged me to incorporate the Electronic Classroom into the class learning process. Not knowing exactly what I was getting into, I decided to get involved.

The Electronic Classroom works through the VAX and is fairly new at IU, and it can be a wonderful pedagogical device. It was a bit daunting to learn how to use it, and students grumbled at first because they had to go to the IU Access Microcomputer Center and get an e-mail account, then learn how to log into VAX. But we all found that it was not so difficult at all once we dove in. The basic idea was that students in my class could enter the VAX and talk with each other about anything. It was terrific. I used it in the following ways:

Self-introduction. They went wild on this, discovering mutual interests, arguing over favorite Chicago radio stations, rock groups, Bloomington Catholic churches, etc. Everyone got into the fray, and it bonded them in a way that two 75 minute classroom sessions could never have done.

Mid-term examination. I gave them a choice of three questions and required them to respond to two other fellow students' answers.

Follow-up on reading week. I gave them a week off to read Steinbeck's East of Eden, which they all loved and which had a huge impact on their interpretation of the biblical text. I asked each student to enter a response limited to two screens and then respond to two other entries. The discussion spread like wild-fire, everyone building on and responding to what all the others had written.

"Whereas the computer is thought to lead to depersonalization, I found just the opposite to be true."

I gave the students study questions in advance on several of the more difficult biblical assignments, to help them prepare for the class discussion. I believe that these questions enhanced the level of class discussion.

All in all, I'm most impressed by the potential of the Electronic Classroom. Whereas the computer is thought to lead to depersonalization, I found just the opposite to be true. It led to the personalization of the learning experience, forming networks of communication that lived on outside of the classroom.

James Ackerman
Religious Studies
IU Bloomington

Electronic Office Hours

Many students avoid professors' office hours, either because they're loathe to disturb a professor or because they fear they'll have to wait in line; sometimes their avoidance is simply the result of diffidence. On campuses with e-mail facilities, electronic office hours are a good way to stay in contact with such students. If you notify students on your syllabus that you'll be on-line at a specific time during the day and that they can VAX you during this period, you can get electronic office hours going. Surprising numbers of students check in during electronic office hours, asking questions that they might not otherwise feel they have the time or the courage to ask. Since posting electronic office hours, I've answered more questions and gotten higher ratings on "availability of the instructor" in formal student evaluations than I used to get holding the equivalent number of regular office hours on campus.

Since posting electronic office hours, I've answered more questions and gotten higher ratings on "availability of the instructor" in formal student evaluations than I used to get holding the equivalent number of regular office hours on campus.

With a modem, you can hold electronic office hours from your home computer. This is actually a lot of fun to do if you're a night owl and you're up in the wee hours, which is when a surprising number of students are active in the computer clusters on campus.

Bonnie Kendall
Anthropology
IU Bloomington

The Electronic Coffee House

Since I've been using the Electronic Classroom feature of our VAX system, I've always tried to allow students a NOTE TOPIC where students can write to each other and where anyone in the class can read their notes and respond to them; it's a kind of bulletin board, but only for me and members of my class. (My colleague, Bob Althauser in Sociology, suggested this and provided the wonderful name "Coffee House.") The conversations in the coffee house can get quite animated and interesting, which means that a lot of students try to visit it at least once a day and make contributions. Students who never talk in class often shine in the coffee house.

Coffee House notes don't always concern themselves with strictly academic topics. Frequently the students are socializing, playing with ideas, making connections, creating community. I've learned more about the composition of my classes through the coffee house than I ever learned from tests and papers.

A colleague at Purdue, where they don't have Electronic Classroom, was nevertheless able to get their academic computing support staff to set up special bulletin boards just for his classes (and even though they thought it was a curious request, they complied). The Purdue students, my friend reports, loved it.

Bonnie Kendall
Anthropology
IU Bloomington

Electronic Dialogue

Dialogue journals may be written with pen and paper, but electronic mail opens even more possibilities for flexibility:

- Students can converse over distance.

- Students can converse and print out a hard copy to record the process of learning.

- As faculty encourage students to be reflective learners and to be involved in their own assessment, a record of the evolution of ideas, successful modes of learning, and collaborative interactions will be invaluable.

- Students and faculty can use such records in their learning and teaching portfolios.

Barbara Cambridge
English/Campus Writing
IUPUI

MOMENTS . . .

What Would You Have Done????

One spring before coming to IU, I had posted my final exam scores and course grades, then gone home to mow my yard. One of my senior students drove up with a car full of friends and relatives for the next day's graduation. He had received a "C" in my class, but he needed a "B" to graduate. His parents were there for graduation; he was to be married the next week assuming his graduation; he had signed a job contract assuming his graduation.

Then his tears gushed out his contact lenses in my freshly mowed grass . . .

He started to cry, then bawl; the story was so touching that even I was tearing up. Then his tears gushed out his contact lenses in my freshly mowed grass; he, his friends, and his relatives spent all afternoon searching through my front yard for the missing contacts. <u>What would you have done?</u>

Cliff Scott
History
IU Fort Wayne

"Put a Shine on Your Shoes"

Fresh out of undergraduate school with a teaching certificate, I was substitute teaching in an inner city school in Decatur, Illinois. I was assigned to an industrial arts class, which to a music teacher was like being assigned to the front line in World War II without a gun. During one class in which they were putting together bird feeders, one student began yelling and threatening another student with a rather large 2 x 4. The other student picked up a lead pipe and proceeded to do the same.

During one class in which they were putting together bird feeders, one student began yelling and threatening another student with a rather large 2 x 4.

My life flashing before my eyes, I got in between the students to stop the fight. Well, being very young, small and very blonde, they turned their anger towards me. Also, it was quite apparent that they had been smoking more than cigarettes before class. Thinking this might be my last performance, I started to tap dance and sing, "Put a Shine on Your Shoes." Surprise and the fact that they thought I was crazy, broke the violent atmosphere. Their anger disappeared and thankfully the bell soon rang.

George Pinney
Theatre & Drama
IU Bloomington

How's It Going?

I was academic advisor to a student who was also enrolled in one of my classes. At midterm, because he had some very low grades in several classes, I called him to my office for the college-mandated "how's it going" session.

He said that he'd cut a lot of classes, including test days.

As we talked, he said that he'd cut a lot of classes, including test days. He said he hadn't been doing much of the reading, even for my class. I tactfully tried to explore what the problem was; I suggested that perhaps it was hard to study in a noisy residence hall, or perhaps he had taken too many classes, or perhaps he needed to sharpen up by taking the study skills class. He responded respectfully, although it was clear that I hadn't quite figured out the problem. So I asked him, "What do you think might help get you through the semester better?" He responded, "Well, I'll tell you the truth, I've had trouble ever since I came to this planet." He wasn't kidding.

Jo Young Switzer
Communication
IU Fort Wayne

CONTRIBUTORS

Kela Adams
Education/
Physical Education
IU Southeast

James Ackerman
Religious Studies
IU Bloomington

Rich Aniskiewicz
Computer Technology
IU Kokomo

Kevin Sue Bailey
Education
IU Southeast

Eileen Bender
English
IU South Bend

Christine Bennett
Multicultural Education
IU Bloomington

Dave Boeyink
Journalism
IU Bloomington

Erwin Boschmann
Faculty Development
IUPUI

Ben Brabson
Physics
IU Bloomington

Carol Browne
Elementary Education
IU East

Barbara Cambridge
English/
Campus Writing
IUPUI

Bernardo Carducci
Psychology
IU Southeast

Kris Dhawale
Chemistry
IU East

Bill Frederick
Computer Science
IP Ft. Wayne

Art Friedel
Chemistry
IU Ft. Wayne

Patrick Furlong
History
IU South Bend

Laura Ginger
Business Law
IU Bloomington

Linda Gugin
Political Science
IU Southeast

Linda Haas
Sociology/
Women's Studies
IUPUI

Sharon Hamilton
English
IUPUI

Archibald Hendry
Physics
IU Bloomington

Luke Johnson
Religious Studies
IU Bloomington

Juanita Keck
Nursing
IUPUI

Mike Keen
Sociology
IU Southeast

Bonnie Kendall
Anthropology
IU Bloomington

Brenda Knowles
Business Law
IU South Bend

Catherine Larson
Spanish and Portuguese
IU Bloomington

George Leddick
Counselor Education
IP Ft. Wayne

Monle Lee
Marketing
IU South Bend

Lowell Madden
Education
IP Ft. Wayne

Jane Mallor
Business Law
IU Bloomington

Robin Morgan
Psychology
IU Southeast

James Mumford
Afro-American
Arts Institute
IU Bloomington

Craig Nelson
Biology
IU Bloomington

Nick Nelson
English
IU Kokomo

Gregor Novak
Physics
IUPUI

Robert Orr
Computer Technology
IUPUI

Robert Otten
English
IU Kokomo

John Peck
Economics
IU South Bend

Bernice Pescosolido
Institute for
Social Research
IU Bloomington

Vince Peterson
Education
IU South Bend

Katherine Phelps
Finance
IU South Bend

George Pinney
Theatre & Drama
IU Bloomington

Gary Potter
Music Theory
IU Bloomington

Richard Powell
Medicine
IUPUI

Jerry Powers
School of Social Work
IUPUI

Eric Richards
Business Law
IU Bloomington

Shirley Rickert
Organizational Leadership and
Supervision
IP Ft. Wayne

Linda Rooda
Nursing
IU Northwest

Patrick Rooney
Economics
IU Columbus

J. Clarke Rountree, III
Rhetorical Studies/
Communication
IU Kokomo

Susan Sciame-Giesecke
Speech Communication
IU Kokomo

Clifford Scott
History
IP Ft. Wayne

Erdogan Sener
Construction
IUPUI

Morteza Shafii-Mousavi
Mathematics
IU South Bend

Susan Shapiro
Psychology
IU East

Margo Sorgman
Social Studies
IU Kokomo

Holly Stocking
Journalism
IU Bloomington

Janet Streepey
Honors Program
IU Bloomington

Jo Young Switzer
Communication
IP Ft. Wayne

Eleanor Turk
History
IU East

Susan VanDyke
Theatre Design
IU Southeast

Bob Votaw
Geology
IU Northwest

Walter Wagor
Psychology
IU East

Marilyn Watkins
Education
IU East

Peggy Wilkes
FACET Coordinator
Nontraditional Student
IU Bloomington

Earl Wysong
Sociology
IU Kokomo

Mimi Zolan
Biology
IU Bloomington